PLAYS BY
ANTHONY CLARVOE

BROADWAY PLAY PUBLISHING INC
224 E 62nd St, NY, NY 10065
www.broadwayplaypub.com
info@broadwayplaypub.com

Cover photo by Peter Cunningham

First printing: January 1996
This printing: August 2016
I S B N: 978-0-88145-117-7

Book design: Marie Donovan
Word processing: Microsoft Word for Windows
Typographic controls: Xerox Ventura Publisher 2.0 P E
Typeface: Palatino
Printed and bound in the U S A.

CONTENTS

ABOUT THE AUTHOR

Anthony Clarvoe was born in San Francisco and lives in New York and the midwest. His first produced play, PICK UP AX (published by B P P I), premiered at the Eureka Theatre in 1990. Since then his plays have been produced by South Coast Repertory, Denver Center Theatre, Repertory Theatre of St Louis, Cincinnati Playhouse in the Park, Northlight Theatre, San Jose Repertory, Empty Space, and many others across the United States.

Clarvoe has received fellowships and grants from the Guggenheim, W Alton Jones, McKnight, and Jerome Foundations; the Fund for New American Plays; and the National Endowment for the Arts, as well as two Drama-Logue Awards and the National Theatre Council's Stavis Award. His most recent script is a new play based on Dostoevsky's THE BROTHERS KARAMAZOV. He is a member of the Writers Guild of America, the Dramatists Guild, and the Playwrights' Center.

A NOTE FROM THE PLAYWRIGHT

These plays were written and rewritten between 1990 and 1993, and had their first productions in the 1992-93 season. To acknowledge fully the contributions of the hundred or so gifted and dedicated artists who took these scripts to the stage would fill another book. Some of them are named in the pages below. In addition, my gratitude to Joan Scott, William Craver, and Marti Blumenthal, and to Erna Clarvoe and Jennifer S Clarvoe, for their support and encouragement.

These plays, as varied as they are, all turn out to be celebrations of learning. My thanks and love to Samuel Scott Clarvoe, the best learner I know.

THE LIVING

THE LIVING was presented as a workshop in the Mark Taper Forum's 1991 New Works Festival, directed by Oskar Eustis; in the Denver Center's U S West TheatreFest '92, directed by Nagle Jackson; in Carnegie Mellon's 1992 Showcase of New Plays, directed by Brian Kulik; and at Kenyon College, directed by Harlene Marley; and in readings at the Oregon Shakepeare Festival, the Playwrights' Center, and Upstart Stage.

The world premiere of THE LIVING was presented on 3 May 1993 by the Denver Center Theater Company, Donovan Marley, Artistic Director, in U S West TheatreFest '93. The cast and creative contributors were:

MR JOHN GRAUNT .... Jamie Horton
MRS SARAH CHANDLER .... Katherine Heasley
DR EDWARD HARMAN .... Sean Hennigan
MRS ELIZABETH FINCH .... Kay Doubleday
SIR JOHN LAWRENCE .... William M Whitehead
LORD BROUNKER .... Michael Santo
REV DR THOMAS VINCENT .... Richard Risso
Ensemble .... Douglas Harmsen, James Baker, Michael Hartman

Director .... Nagle Jackson
Set .... Vicki Smith
Lighting .... Charles R MacLeod
Costumes .... Lyndall L Otto
Sound .... Joel Underwood
Stage manager .... Christopher C Ewing

ACKNOWLEDGMENTS

The events that took place in London in 1665 have survived thanks to the extraordinary testimony left by Captain John Graunt, Nathaniel Hodges, M D, Sir John Lawrence, the Reverend Dr Simon Patrick, Mr Samuel Pepys, and the Reverend Dr Thomas Vincent; and to a remarkable act of historical imagination, Daniel Defoe's novel A JOURNAL OF THE PLAGUE YEAR. This script owes a handful of sentences, and its existence, to them.

Dozens of directors, actors, designers, dramaturgs, crew, and staff worked with uncommon dedication to bring THE LIVING into being. My particular thanks to Nagle Jackson, Oskar Eustis, Brian Kulick, Harlene Marley, and Tom Szentgyorgyi.

My thanks also to the Fund for New American Plays and the W Alton Jones Foundation for their generous financial support for THE LIVING.

CHARACTERS

Mr John Graunt, early thirties, a scientist
Mrs Sarah Chandler, late twenties, a shopkeeper's wife
Dr Edward Harman, mid-thirties, a physician
Mrs Elizabeth Finch, early forties, a searcher of the dead
Sir John Lawrence, late forties, Lord Mayor, a merchant
Lord Brounker, early fifties, a cavalier
Rev Dr Thomas Vincent, thirties, a nonconformist minister

Three men, twenties to forties, may play the following roles:

Man 1: Mr Sawyer, a cabinetmaker
Paul, Sarah's brother, a shopkeeper
Lawrence's Clerk
First Constable
Robert, a smith from Walthamstow

Man 2: Mr Mills, an Anglican minister
Second Constable
Brounker's Clerk
Andrew, a shopkeeper from Walthamstow

Man 3: Dr Goddard, a physician
Jamey, a watchman
Bill, a farmer from Walthamstow

SCENE

London, 1665

SET

A lower level and a slightly raised upper level connected by steps. A few pieces of furniture come and go, but the stage is as bare as possible.

A NOTE ON STAGING

Throughout the action, until the very end, no one approaches within arm's reach of anyone else. The exception is HARMAN, and only when he wears protective clothing. No object is handed directly from one person to another. Everyone on stage is isolated in space.

For if they fall, the one will lift up his fellow:
but woe to him that is alone when he falleth;
for he hath not another to help him up.

Ecclesiastes 4:10

ACT ONE

Scene One

(On the steps: SARAH *sits on one side, head on her arms.* GRAUNT *stands on the other side, holding a large sheet of paper, densely printed. He looks up.)*

GRAUNT: Ague and Fever, 5,257. Chrisomes and Infants, 1,258. Consumption and Tissick, 4,808.

*(*GRAUNT *turns upstage to look at:)*

(On the upper level: DOCTOR HARMAN, *wearing a protective suit which completely hides his features. He hovers around a cot with a still figure in it. The suit includes a bulbous headpiece that covers him to the neck. A long breathing tube, shaped much like a bird's beak, protrudes from the front. He wears long, heavy gloves and a floor-length cloak. The whole suit is black and he looks, in sum, like a giant crow wearing a tricorn hat.)*

*(*GRAUNT *turns back.)*

GRAUNT: This is a publication that comes out every week. Has for sixty years now. Each parish reports: how many christened, how many died, what they died of. It's called the Bills of Mortality. People subscribe, glance through. At year's end, they publish a summary. Convulsion, 2,036. Dropsy and Timpany, 1,478.

*(*HARMAN *pulls a sheet over the body and crosses down the steps near, but not too near,* SARAH. *He pulls off his bird head.* HARMAN *speaks to* SARAH, *who nods.)*

GRAUNT: Frighted, 23. Grief, 46. Overlaid and Starved, 45. Plague, 110,596.

*(*HARMAN *exits.)*

GRAUNT: We did not know where it came from. We did not know what caused it. We had no way to stop it. For all we knew, it would never end. For all we knew, the world would end, in 1665. Bear that in mind. Judge what we did. For in this account it does not matter what becomes of me, or any of us. All that matters is what becomes of you. And what we did may be of use to you, if this ever should happen again. *(He exits.)*

FINCH: *(Off)* Sarah? Sarah?

(MRS FINCH *enters. She carries a white wand, the badge of office of a searcher of the dead.*)

FINCH: There you are. No, stay where you are, dear.

SARAH: I should get you something.

FINCH: No.

SARAH: Mrs Finch, come in and may I offer you something? I'll call the boy to go around, I don't know what there is in the house.

FINCH: Is everyone gone, then? No, don't you move. I'll just see him and be gone.

SARAH: He's all right. Everyone says he's all right.

FINCH: Where are the children?

SARAH: My sister has them.

FINCH: How are they?

SARAH: They're all right. Everyone's all right here. Truly.

FINCH: I should see him. Then we'd know.

SARAH: No, really, you don't have to.

FINCH: I do, though, you know. Won't take a moment.

SARAH: Can't you just leave him alone?

FINCH: Sarah, the parish needs to know what he had. What are the parish clerks going to do all day if they can't be writing down all the babies born and who their parents are and the dead and what their sickness was?

SARAH: The doctor said it was spotted fever.

FINCH: Did he?

SARAH: Yes. He did. So I don't see why you have to --

FINCH: Rumor.

SARAH: I don't underst —what rumor?

FINCH: You hear two houses have been shut up in Chancery Lane?

SARAH: I didn't know— I've been at his bedside here—

FINCH: Whole household locked in. A rumor got around they had the plague. (*Pause*) Believe me, you're lucky it's me that's here. When my husband died they sent an old drunk woman, some old drunkard I barely knew barged into my home to tell me what killed my man was the apoplexy. And it wasn't apoplexy, it was heart, as everyone said, as the doctor said, but she saw a red face and said apoplexy, and there he is in the register, now to the Day of Judgment, dead of apoplexy. Till he rise again and straighten it out.

SARAH: Everyone said spotted fever, Mrs Finch, ask anyone.

FINCH: Not everyone, Sarah. What they say is one thing, but where have they gone?

SARAH: He's gone. There's nothing more to do here.

FINCH: Nothing? And no one to gather around you, grieving alone?

SARAH: They left because he's gone. That's all. He's gone.

FINCH: And they didn't want to go with him. But your children are all right?

SARAH: They've been with my sister.

FINCH: I should drop around there.

SARAH: I didn't let them touch him. I didn't let the children touch him, I didn't let his sister touch him or his mother touch him or anyone, no one touched him at all.

FINCH: Lonely death. No one there.

SARAH: I was there.

FINCH: Touching him.

SARAH: Sometimes.

FINCH: And now you'll want to see your children. And touch them, too. So you see? It's important what people know.

SARAH: Would we have to be quarantined?

FINCH: Only if it's the plague.

SARAH: It's not.

FINCH: That's what I'm here to decide. (Pause) Now, if you like, when I visit the children— for which the parish gives me not a thing, this is my concern as a neighbor now— if there's something you'd like me...to take for them?

SARAH: A message?

FINCH: A message, yes, but even if you had something you wanted me to take. For them. For their comfort? To make sure they *stay* comfortable? (Pause) Isn't that what we all want, Sarah, that the children be comfortable and safe?

SARAH: Mrs Finch. There is something? If you could?

FINCH: Is there?

SARAH: If you could...keep it for me?

FINCH: If that's what you'd like.

SARAH: We've been saving it. To keep the wolf from the door. But now—it's not a lot.

FINCH: That's fine. I know you, Sarah, you're a good girl. *(She crosses up the steps past SARAH.)* And now I'll have a quick look—

SARAH: Spotted fever, it's— he ran a fever, and— red spots, and— everyone said— *everyone* said. Before they went away.

(FINCH peers at the figure in the cot and crosses quickly back down the steps.)

FINCH: What do you know. Spotted fever.

SARAH: Is— is it?

FINCH: Now you know.

SARAH: Is it really? The children—

FINCH: Now if you'll tell me where you've got that little something—

SARAH: Let me get it for you—

FINCH: No! Stay where you are.

(The lights fade on SARAH and FINCH as:)

Scene Two

(Clamorous voices just offstage)

VOICES: *(Off)* I'm the next one in!
I don't care if he's in there!
I'll wait!

(On the lower level: Lights up as four men enter, at a cautious distance from each other. The first three have handkerchiefs over their faces and are wearing heavy cloaks. The last is GRAUNT who, as he crosses, comes too close to MAN 2.)

MAN 2: Watch yourself!

GRAUNT: Sorry.

MAN 1: *(Furthest into the room)* Give a man some breathing room, could you?

MAN 2: *(In the middle of the room)* All you want.

(MAN 2 moves further from MAN 1.)

MAN 3: Watch it!

MAN 2: Look, I've got him on the other side as well.

MAN 3: There's other rooms you could wait in.

MAN 2: Not if you want a pass. I came here for a pass.

MAN 1: You can wait the same as anyone.

(LAWRENCE *enters.*)

ALL: Sir! Sir John!

LAWRENCE: All right. Who is next?

ALL: Here!

LAWRENCE: Does everyone have a certificate of health from the College of Physicians?

MEN 2 AND 3: Yes! Here!

MAN 2: Cost me enough.

MAN 1: Wait! They told me I had to go here first!

LAWRENCE: You're mistaken.

MAN 3: Got you good, son.

MAN 1: That's what they told me!

GRAUNT: Sir?

LAWRENCE: Anyone who wants a pass to leave London must go to the College for examination and return with a certificate of health.

MAN 1: Listen!

MAN 2: Clear out, would you?

LAWRENCE: I must have a certificate—

MAN 3: Here! Got mine here!

GRAUNT: Sir?

LAWRENCE: You, step forward.

MAN 2: Hey!

MAN 3: Thank you! Certificate, right here!

(MAN 3 *crosses toward* LAWRENCE *and places his certificate on the desk. He backs away and* LAWRENCE *looks at it without touching it, signs a piece of paper, places it next to the certificate, and backs away while* MAN 3 *crosses to the desk and takes the certificate and the pass, all during the following:)*

MAN 1: Friend? That certificate?

MAN 2: What of it?

MAN 1: How much for it?

MAN 2: Sorry, friend, I'm through dealing in them, I've saved this for myself.

LAWRENCE: Next!

MAN 1: Please.

MAN 2: Try outside. Certificate here!

LAWRENCE: You! How many are in the outer room?

MAN 3: Dozens.

GRAUNT: Fifty-three, actually.

LAWRENCE: Tell them to obey the constables and they'll all get a turn!

(MAN 2 *and* LAWRENCE *go through the same routine.*)

MAN 3: Hail and farewell, all!

MAN 1: Friend?

MAN 2: Thank you, Sir John!

(MAN 2 *exits.*)

MAN 1: That pass. You want to be careful who hears you have it. Thieves around.

MAN 3: Oh. Thanks. Well, I'm—

GRAUNT: Sir?

VOICES: *(Off)* Make way!

BROUNKER: *(Off)* Clear away there!

MAN 1: Why don't we go along together? Safety in numbers.

MAN 3: But you haven't got a pass yet.

MAN 1: Oh, I'll get one somehow. Coming?

VOICE: *(Off)* Clear a path for Lord Brounker!

(LORD BROUNKER *enters. Everyone bows.*)

BROUNKER: Hey ho, Jack.

LAWRENCE: Good morning, my Lord.

(MEN 1 *and* 3 *exit.*)

BROUNKER: No formalities, Jack, honestly, times like these.

LAWRENCE: It's good to see you, Harry. I'd started to think I was the only one left.

BROUNKER: I'm here on the King's business. Got your family out?

LAWRENCE: All out, settled in the country place.

BROUNKER: What about yourself? When do you go?

LAWRENCE: I'll be staying here.

BROUNKER: Jesus! Can't you leave it to the aldermen or something?

LAWRENCE: Harry. I'm an alderman.

BROUNKER: You're the Lord Mayor! Why can't you run things from a distance? Privy Council is.

LAWRENCE: Are they running things, or are they just running?

BROUNKER: Ho, Jack, gently now. All the best people are leaving.

LAWRENCE: What does that make you and me and the aldermen?

BROUNKER: The aldermen are excellent fellows, Jack, but surely you're a cut above them. We think of you as one of us. His Majesty himself, just before he left for Salisbury, said, "No one I'd rather have on the job than bully Jack Lawrence." He wants to know everything you do. I'm to be his eyes and ears.

LAWRENCE: Splendid, Harry! Who else is staying?

BROUNKER: Well, Albemarle is staying. But, Jack—

LAWRENCE: The Duke of Albemarle is upriver in Westminster.

BROUNKER: You don't want to work with him anyway. His physician told him the best preventive for the plague is a gallon of whiskey a day. He'll be drunk for the duration.

LAWRENCE: Aren't any of the Privy Council going to stay?

BROUNKER: Why do you need that pack of political lapdogs underfoot?

LAWRENCE: We'll need every figure of authority we can get. Together we may do this.

BROUNKER: Do what, exactly?

LAWRENCE: Harry. If all the best people are leaving, then all the worst people must be staying. They could riot in the streets any day. They might decide to loot your house.

BROUNKER: Ah. Can't the sheriffs keep them down?

LAWRENCE: They'll be no match for a mob.

BROUNKER: Call in the army.

LAWRENCE: It's a funny thing about armies. If you stand back and ask them to march into a plague they tend to resent you. They tend to become a mob. And so you have two mobs, and one of them has weapons.

BROUNKER: Ah.

LAWRENCE: The first thing we do is tell the Privy Council that we need enough money to keep the live people fed, the dying people indoors, and the dead people buried.

VOICES: *(Off)* Please! Sir! Can you give me a certificate, Sir!

GODDARD: *(Off)* I have business with the Lord Mayor!

VOICES: *(Off)* So do I!

GODDARD: *(Off)* I am with the College of Physicians!

LAWRENCE: Let him in!

(GODDARD *and* SAWYER *enter.* GODDARD *is wearing a protective suit like* HARMAN's. SAWYER *carries a roll of paper and measuring tools.* GODDARD *pulls off his headpiece.)*

GODDARD: Madness, madness.

LAWRENCE: Doctor Goddard. Good of you to come.

GODDARD: Good day, Sir John, the College has met and I have brought the proposed design.

BROUNKER: Goddard! Splendid, just the man—

GODDARD: Lord Brounker! What a surprise!

BROUNKER: Now I need your advice—

GODDARD: But, my Lord, I thought—

BROUNKER: This is about another matter.

(LAWRENCE *has noticed that* SAWYER *is sighting down his thumb at him.)*

LAWRENCE: Young man? May I help you?

GODDARD: Mr Sawyer will be taking your dimensions.

LAWRENCE: Goddard, why does the College of Physicians think that standing inside a box is going to keep me healthy?

BROUNKER: Hey what?

LAWRENCE: They want to display me in a glass cabinet, like a waxwork.

GODDARD: The wood and glass will interpose themselves between you and the contagious air your petitioners breathe at you. It is the same principle as the headpieces we doctors are wearing.

BROUNKER: Doesn't that scare the hell out of your patients?

GODDARD: The beak filters the infected air.

BROUNKER: And makes you look rather like a vulture.

GODDARD: Sir John, would you care to see the rendering of the box?

LAWRENCE: Please.

(SAWYER *unrolls the drawing and holds it up.*)

LAWRENCE: Jesus. I look like a prisoner in the dock.

GODDARD: If you want any modifications...

LAWRENCE: Give me some room to maneuver in there. A place to sit.

GODDARD: Note all this, would you, Sawyer?

LAWRENCE: A slot to pass papers in and out. A chamber pot. It'll save a little time.

BROUNKER: Goddard? If no air comes in—

GODDARD: Exactly, my Lord. The contagion—

BROUNKER: And no air goes out....

(*Pause*)

GODDARD: Air holes.

SAWYER: Hm.

GODDARD: Thank you, my Lord. Sawyer, sketch out a new design.

BROUNKER: Now listen, Goddard. Tell me what to do. I ordered a new suit a few weeks ago, beautiful silk, apple-blossom shade— you'd appreciate it, Jack, wasn't haberdashery how you made your pile?— friend in the haberdashers guild put me onto the silk, Thomason—

LAWRENCE: Ah yes—

BROUNKER: —took me down to the docks, pulled it right out of the crates for me, silk the color of apple blossom, floating in the breeze off the Thames. All the fittings, I'd slip it on and swear I could feel that breeze. Marvelous stuff. I sent the silk to my tailor—

LAWRENCE: Who does your— ?

BROUNKER: Meredith, well, and there's the difficulty. I took delivery today, and I've just heard he's fallen ill.

GODDARD: Plague?

BROUNKER: Maybe, maybe not, "fallen ill," that's all you hear anymore.

LAWRENCE: That's a shame. He does beautiful work. When do we see you wear the suit?

BROUNKER: Wear it? I'm afraid to have the damn thing in the house. Am I being stupid here?

GODDARD: My Lord is right to be cautious.

BROUNKER: I've told my man not to hang it in the wardrobe for fear of infecting the rest of my clothes.

GODDARD: Have your man fumigate it overnight in a fire made of sea coal.

BROUNKER: I can't visit his majesty smelling like a campfire.

GODDARD: It would be best not to wear the suit till the plague is past. By then the contagion should have faded.

BROUNKER: By then the fashion will have changed. *(He looks at the clothes he's wearing.)* He did do good work, didn't he. What a fucking waste.

VOICES: *(Off)* Hey! Wait your turn!

MILLS: *(Off)* I am a Doctor of Divinity!

LAWRENCE: Let him in!

BROUNKER: Is it always like this?

(MILLS enters.)

LAWRENCE: On the slow days.

MILLS: Sweet Jesus.

LAWRENCE: Good morning, Reverend Mills.

MILLS: Sir John, I have been inspecting the parishes as you asked?

BROUNKER: Hm?

LAWRENCE: We warn them that public gatherings are unhealthy, and they insist on praying together.

BROUNKER: Commendable, really. Stupid, but commendable.

LAWRENCE: Is there any means to keep the people away?

MILLS: From church? But, Sir John—

BROUNKER: Make the sermons more boring.

GODDARD: Impossible.

BROUNKER: True.

MILLS: I found most of the churches have no ministers. They seem to be leaving the city.

LAWRENCE: I don't believe it.

MILLS: Almost none of us are left.

BROUNKER: I thought London was lousy with preachers. Didn't we appoint cartloads of you people when we gave the fucking Puritans the toss?

LAWRENCE: First the court goes, now the clergy. Jesus, this town feels empty now all the cowards are leaving.

(*Pause*)

BROUNKER: The King has left London. Sir.

(*Pause*)

LAWRENCE: The King is the body of England. He has a duty to preserve himself.

BROUNKER: The man has a stallion's courage—

GODDARD: Stayed in town for weeks after the first case broke out—

BROUNKER: And a fucking magnificent king he is, gentlemen—

MILLS: Amen—

BROUNKER: Like a horse, God's my witness. Lady Castlemayne is swelling by the day, the ladies-in-waiting are pleading exhaustion— just to keep him from catching the pox, his physician has invented the cleverest little device.

GODDARD: I've heard. Ingenious man, Doctor Condom.

MILLS: Actually, I had intended to stay.

BROUNKER: Had you.

LAWRENCE: I am very pleased to hear it.

BROUNKER: Yes. How soldierly of you.

MILLS: And I pray many times a day that God maintain my resolve. Look at this.

(MILLS *pulls out a flier and places it on* LAWRENCE's *desk.*)

LAWRENCE: "Vacant churches for rent. Best offer accepted."

MILLS: My Lord, there has been an outbreak of satire.

LAWRENCE: Who is responsible?

MILLS: Dissenters and nonconformists. They are starting to return.

BROUNKER: Strictly illegal. Put them down, Jack. We're still running the prison ships. We'll crate them all up and dump them in America.

LAWRENCE: We'll arrest the leaders to start with. I'll try and talk sense to them. Thank you, Reverend Mills. Good day.

MILLS: Good day, Sir John. Good day, my Lord.

LAWRENCE: Mills. I thank God you are staying.

MILLS: Yes. May he grant me the strength.

LAWRENCE: Yes.

MILLS: As long as I possibly can. *(He exits.)*

LAWRENCE: I give him a week.

BROUNKER: You might as well give him a pass out of town right now.

GODDARD: Rightly so. I am sending all my patients to Salisbury with his majesty.

LAWRENCE: But, Goddard—

GODDARD: The air in the country is wholesome and fresh. A sovereign shield against distemper. The necessities of life in such times as these are more plentiful there, and there are just— fewer troubles in general. If we disperse, the plague passes over an empty place and the people can return when the weather turns healthy again.

LAWRENCE: Goddard. We have great need of physicians now.

GODDARD: Oh, I will do anything in my power for my patients. Do anything and go anywhere.

LAWRENCE: Splendid.

GODDARD: I would follow them to the ends of the earth, if necessary. And as my patients are almost exclusively attached to the court, I find I really have to go to Salisbury.

LAWRENCE: What about the people who are staying behind?

GODDARD: Who would that be?

LAWRENCE: Servants minding their masters' property. Laborers whose employers have shut their doors. Anyone who works for a living, and whose only work is here. The poor. Harry and I have to keep them from panicking. What will they do when they hear that the doctors have run?

GODDARD: Every physician I know has signed his own certificate of health and is packing to leave. What do you want us to do?

LAWRENCE: I want you to think of something. While you wait for your pass to be signed.

(Pause)

BROUNKER: Jack, you old horse trader.

GODDARD: Very well, Sir. The College of Physicians shall provide, free of charge, a list of preventives for the plague. We shall engage our chief apothecary to remain here and dispense medicines.

LAWRENCE: At the College's expense.

GODDARD: Agreed.

LAWRENCE: I need doctors. Talk to the College. I'll pay them at the public charge if I have to.

BROUNKER: Just a moment. Are you proposing that the government pay for medical care?

LAWRENCE: Harry, if we could talk about the means of payment later—

GODDARD: If money is forthcoming, we should find a few volunteers.

LAWRENCE: We'll find your money.

GODDARD: That would have to include pensions for their survivors.

LAWRENCE: Done.

GODDARD: Done. Good day then. My Lord, may I call on you in Salisbury? Your man came by for your certificate of health, I trust you received it?

LAWRENCE: Harry?

BROUNKER: Thank you, yes, I believe I have.

GODDARD: Good day, my Lord.

(*As* GODDARD *exits, the hubbub outside rises.*)

LAWRENCE: Harry...oh, Christ Almighty! (*He crosses to the door.*) All of you! Out! Come back in an hour!

(LAWRENCE *turns to* BROUNKER *as the hubbub subsides.*)

BROUNKER: The King wants me with him.

LAWRENCE: I thought you were here on his business.

BROUNKER: Not to stay.

LAWRENCE: Why can't you stay here? Travel down there.

BROUNKER: If I stayed here, they'd never receive me down there, would they.

LAWRENCE: I thought you were his majesty's eyes and ears.

BROUNKER: I am. And he doesn't want his eyes and ears to become diseased. When I come for your reports we're to meet on the outskirts of town. You'll be the hero, you know. Do your duty, and it's glory and everything. My duty, it seems, is to anticipate the King's desires and keep him amused.

LAWRENCE: Much in the manner of Lady Castlemayne.

(*Pause*)

BROUNKER: In the manner of a cavalier. And a friend of the King.

LAWRENCE: Why would he risk such a friend on a job like this?

BROUNKER: Well, because I insisted, didn't I. Had to do something.

LAWRENCE: Damn it, Harry, you're a good man, I need you here.

BROUNKER: To do what? What do you think you'll be doing? Giving the scum of the city titles like searchers of the dead and watchers of houses? Sharing the latest gossip, "So-and-so is dying, Such-and-such is dead?" Watching the bodies be buried? My God, man, you can't trust the clothes on your back!

(LAWRENCE *signs a pass.*)

BROUNKER: I'll tell them the city needs money.

LAWRENCE: I'll ask the aldermen to estimate their needs.

(BROUNKER *crosses to the desk and picks up the pass.*)

BROUNKER: How many of the aldermen did you persuade to stay?

LAWRENCE: We had a meeting together over that.

BROUNKER: Are any of them staying?

LAWRENCE: All of them are staying.

(*Pause*)

BROUNKER: Each of us to his duty, then. (*He turns to go.*)

LAWRENCE: Would you— please tell his majesty I shall do everything I can to preserve his city. Tell him we are praying for him.

BROUNKER: He will pray for you as well. You in particular, Jack. (*He exits.*)

LAWRENCE: Did you hear that, Mr Sawyer? My name in the King's prayers. Imagine that.

SAWYER: Aye, it's all who you know.... Do you want to see this sketch, Sir John?

LAWRENCE: Yes, all right.

SAWYER: I'm afraid the additional wood will be very dear.

LAWRENCE: Here we go. Disaster is a sellers' market.

SAWYER: I'm stocking all the planks I can get my hands on now, Sir.

LAWRENCE: Why on earth?

SAWYER: Well, for the coffins.

LAWRENCE: Damn it, this isn't a coffin you're building me!

SAWYER: No, Sir. Quite the opposite. (*He holds up a new sketch.*) I put the air holes in the back, away from the people you'll be meeting.

LAWRENCE: Mr Sawyer, am I going to be able to hear people through this thing?

SAWYER: Well, Sir, if I build it to specifications...no.

LAWRENCE: So people will talk and talk and they'll watch me smiling and nodding and I won't hear a word they say.

SAWYER: Very likely, Sir.

LAWRENCE: I'll be just like a politician. Thank you all the same.

SAWYER: Sir John...I have spent some time on this.

LAWRENCE: Here. Here's for your time.

(LAWRENCE *reaches into his wallet and holds out a coin.* SAWYER *hesitates.* LAWRENCE *puts the coin down on his desk.* SAWYER *covers his hand with a rag and picks up the coin.*)

SAWYER: Sir John? Good luck, Sir. *(He exits.)*

(Pause)

LAWRENCE: And what the hell do you want?

(This to GRAUNT, *who has been in the room all this time.)*

GRAUNT: Oh. Graunt. My name is John Graunt. Sir.

LAWRENCE: I suppose you want a pass out of town.

GRAUNT: Oh. No, actually. Too much to do here.

LAWRENCE: You mean you're not essential to the King?

GRAUNT: Well. Not essential, not yet. Known to him though. He made me a Fellow of the Royal Society.

LAWRENCE: Congratulations.

GRAUNT: Thank you, yes. They're all gentlemen dilettantes, really, but I'm only a tradesman, so who am I to talk. Not all dilettantes, in fairness, a few men of knowledge in there. Newton might come up with something. Do you know him, Isaac Newton, no, of course you wouldn't, promising boy, teaches maths at Cambridge, anyway, Royal Society, great honor, a year, no, two years ago, my book came out three years ago, 1662, so two years now.

LAWRENCE: And what moved his majesty to honor you?

GRAUNT: I think because I proved that if there were a plague it wouldn't be his fault.

LAWRENCE: Yes, I expect that was it.

GRAUNT: It was just a matter of looking at the Bills of Mortality.

LAWRENCE: I look at the Bills, everyone looks at the Bills.

GRAUNT: No, actually, you don't. No one does. Or did. Till me. Look. Take the plague. What does everyone think about the plague?

LAWRENCE: I find that for the most part they oppose it.

GRAUNT: You do?

LAWRENCE: Don't you?

GRAUNT: I don't see anyone preventing it, so no. Now. What does everyone think? Either that you can't predict when the plague will happen, or that it happens every twenty years like clockwork. Except for his majesty's enemies, who say that it's broken out whenever one of his dynastic line has been crowned. Judgment of God, you see.

LAWRENCE: And you proved his enemies wrong.

GRAUNT: I proved everybody wrong. If you really look at the Bills, you see there've been plague years after some coronations but not others, you see there is no twenty-year cycle—

LAWRENCE: You see there's no predicting it.

GRAUNT: You see there is. I predicted this one.

LAWRENCE: You did?

GRAUNT: Three years ago. The plague doesn't come from nowhere, you can see it coming months away. Before the plague years, there is always a sickly year: increase of fevers, increase of stillbirths, increase of infant deaths. Same this time.

LAWRENCE: Do you know why that happens?

GRAUNT: Because everyone lies. The plague is there, but they call it different things. Enough searchers lie, and enough parish clerks lie— everything fine in our parish, thank you!— and the government believes them because it wants to, and when the rumors start, they publish items in the *News* and the *Intelligencer* saying it's nothing, and people believe it because they want to. The surest symptom of the approach of the plague is a dramatic increase in lying. Didn't you look at the Bills last year?

LAWRENCE: Well, yes, but...

GRAUNT: You should have looked harder. (*Pause*) Look at the Bills from the previous plagues. Where do they start? In the parishes built on swamp land, bad water, bad drainage, laystalls and slaughterhouses. This plague? The same thing. They put me in the Royal Society, so I thought they believed me, but they only believed me about how it wouldn't be a judgment from God on the King. I've come to ask you a favor. Could I examine the reports from the parish clerks, the numbers that go into the Bills of Mortality?

LAWRENCE: What are you looking for?

GRAUNT: Which direction the plague is spreading, how fast, when it's going to arrive in any given district.

LAWRENCE: So you're a soothsayer.

GRAUNT: No. If you really look at numbers, they'll tell you a story. But no one looks. The King doesn't even know what he's king of.

LAWRENCE: England.

GRAUNT: But nobody knows who that is.

LAWRENCE: Can you really learn those things?

GRAUNT: If I do, will you act on it? Or would you use it to prove that whatever happens isn't your fault?

LAWRENCE: Who's left for me to prove it to? The Lord Mayorship was a ceremonial post, until today. Now I'm running the place. Me, two sheriffs, a handful of clerks and constables, every one of my aldermen, and the goddamn Duke of Albemarle, to run the city of London, and oh, by the bye, there's a plague.

GRAUNT: Sir John, this won't be the end of the world. If someone stays here looking, really looking. We might help, the next time.

LAWRENCE: And you plan to stay in London? Aren't you afraid?

GRAUNT: What, of catching the plague? No, no, I'm just here observing. May I look at the numbers?

LAWRENCE: Come with me. You said you were a tradesman?

GRAUNT: Yes.

LAWRENCE: What do you call your trade?

GRAUNT: I call it statistics. Do you think it might catch on?

(LAWRENCE *and* GRAUNT *exit as the lights crossfade to:*)

Scene Three

(*On the lower level: light through high windows. One by one, a crowd enters.*)

(THOMAS VINCENT *stands on the steps, center.*)

VINCENT: All of our days, until this day, we have had in our ears the whispers of God. He has murmured to us our sweetest thoughts and sung to us our dreams. And all of our days we have stopped our ears. So this day God has raised His voice, and the plague is as a roaring in the street.

To whom is God speaking? To the stricken? Some have told us that our neighbor's illness is the sign of his sin, and that the sick are greater sinners than the healthy. But when we see so many good people die, many while comforting others, can we believe this? No. The righteous die of the same disease as the most profane. We are all buried in the same grave, and sleep there together, till the morning when we rise and go our ways.

(On the lower level: Two CONSTABLES *enter and stand at the back of the crowd.)*

VINCENT: All of London suffers, stricken and well, and we will not suffer alone. The beauty, strength, riches of the whole kingdom lie here. So if the plague is God's sentence, it must be on the whole of our nation. And if this judgment is national, we must reason that national sins have brought it on. That there was a plague upon the heart of this nation long before the plague upon its body. Brothers and sisters, the constables are here.

(The crowd turns to look at the CONSTABLES. *No one moves from his place.)*

CONSTABLE: Are you Thomas Vincent, formerly minister of this parish?

VINCENT: Yes.

CONSTABLE: Will you come with us, please?

VINCENT: This congregation has asked me to speak.

CONSTABLE: You must come with us now.

(The CONSTABLES *take a step closer. The crowd does not move.)*

VINCENT: Brothers and sisters, do not interfere with these men in their duty. Do not touch them. Do not do anything which might risk infecting them.

(The CONSTABLES *stop dead. Pause.)*

VINCENT: If our nation were a person, could he stand trial before the throne without terror? Has our nation been merciful? Has our nation been charitable? Has our nation been peaceable to its neighbors? Has it lacked greed? Has it lacked overweening pride? What kind of person is an empire? Is it entitled to the mercy of God? Does it deserve—

CONSTABLE: Sir, you are under arrest!

VINCENT: Not before I finish my thought! God forgive me, I am angry, I so wanted not to be angry by now. So you see: Constables watch our gates, and watch our streets, and watch our houses. But who can keep watch over his heart, what comes in, and what goes forth? On this day any of you may be taken under arrest by death. I beseech you that hear these words to compare them with the opinion of your conscience. Listen, consider, and lay to heart. God bless you, go in peace. Gentlemen?

(The crowd parts as VINCENT *passes through and exits. The* CONSTABLES *follow warily. The crowd disperses as the lights crossfade to:)*

Scene Four

(On the steps: JAMEY, *a watchman, is sitting in* SARAH's *doorway.* SARAH *stands on the lower level, facing him at a distance.)*

SARAH: I have a right to see inside my house.

JAMEY: No you don't.

SARAH: I want to see my family.

JAMEY: Won't do any good to look at them.

SARAH: I need to know they're all right.

JAMEY: Tell them to lean out the windows. As long as they don't spit onto the street I don't mind.

SARAH: Mary! Paul! *(To* JAMEY*)* Who told the parish my family was infected? Nobody should have said.... It isn't true.

JAMEY: The parish hired me to watch the house, that's all. I've watched other houses.

SARAH: Mary! Paul! Somebody! *(To* JAMEY*)* When will you stop watching this house? When are you going to go away?

JAMEY: When everyone inside stays healthy for two weeks.

SARAH: Two weeks!

JAMEY: Every time another one gets sick, we have to start the calendar again.

SARAH: That could take forever.

JAMEY: That isn't what usually happens.

SARAH: What usually happens?

JAMEY: Everybody dies.

SARAH: Mary!

(On the upper level: PAUL *enters. He stands at the edge of the platform near* JAMEY.*)*

PAUL: Sarah.

SARAH: Paul! How are they?

PAUL: They're sleeping. Everyone's fine. Mary's put the children down for the afternoon, be quiet.

SARAH: They're fine? They're all healthy?

PAUL: The doctor came, everyone's fine.

SARAH: Oh, God. Oh, thank God. Let me see them?

PAUL: They've been bouncing off the walls all day, Sarah, don't wake them up.

SARAH: Are they sleeping all right— we'd finally gotten Becca to sleep through the night, then all this— is she having nightmares?— Is Chris behaving, she promised me she'd help Mary with the little ones— is Georgie taking a bottle?

PAUL: They're eating, they're sleeping, they're fine. Really.

SARAH: (To JAMEY) Damn it, you, my children are in there.

JAMEY: Nice language.

SARAH: Are you going to let me in?

JAMEY: You really want to go in there? To stay?

PAUL: Sarah, don't get locked in here with us.

SARAH: What have they done, that you treat them like this?

JAMEY: They got sick.

SARAH: No.

JAMEY: They might.

SARAH: Anyone in London might be sick for Christ's sake, I might be, you might be.

JAMEY: Yes.

SARAH: So who are you keeping my family from infecting?

JAMEY: The healthy people.

SARAH: Who are the healthy people?

JAMEY: The people who pay me. You don't like the rule, talk to the aldermen.

SARAH: How much?

JAMEY: What?

SARAH: How much are you paid? I'll pay you more.

PAUL: Sarah.

JAMEY: Really?

SARAH: Yes. Tell me what you're paid. I'll double it.

JAMEY: Three watchmen were set in the stocks and beaten this week for letting people escape sick houses.

PAUL: Sarah, don't do this. The man has to live.

SARAH: What am I supposed to do?

PAUL: We need you to keep the trade going.

SARAH: There is no trade, the town's emptying out.

PAUL: Go with them, go to the trading towns.

SARAH: I can't leave the children—

PAUL: Well, you can't hang about on the street.

SARAH: They've already lost their father!

(JAMEY *edges further away from her.*)

SARAH: If I go away what if they think— I'll never see them again?

PAUL: They miss you terribly, but Mary's taking good care of them. Get out of the city, find somewhere safe to trade. If this goes on, we'll need more money to keep the children fed.

SARAH: Is this one getting what you need?

PAUL: We're eating all right. It's just the waiting.

SARAH: Don't just guard them, you turd. Keep them in food.

JAMEY: Nice with the names, thank you.

SARAH: *(To* PAUL*)* I have to see them. Why won't you let me see them?

PAUL: You'll only upset them. We're not supposed to get upset, the doctor said.

SARAH: You're all fine?

PAUL: Yes.

SARAH: Can I bring you anything?

PAUL: Nothing.

SARAH: You swear you're all healthy. Swear to me!

PAUL: I swear to you.

SARAH: I'll triple it. Triple your pay.

JAMEY: Would you tell her to go?

PAUL: Go, Sarah! Don't make it worse.

(Pause)

SARAH: Could you tell Mary— when Becca has a nightmare, if she could rub her back, sometimes it helps, and tell her— tell Mary that Georgie, if she wants to wean him to solid food that's fine because tell her I think my milk's dried up....

(Pause)

PAUL: Stay well, Sarah.

SARAH: And you. *(Pause)* Tell the children I'm well? *(She exits.)*

JAMEY: Called me a turd. Is that nice? *(He takes an apple from his pocket, examines it closely, and takes a bite.)* She's your sister, is she?

PAUL: My wife's sister.

JAMEY: Your wife talk like that?

PAUL: What *do* they pay you? *I'll* triple it. Name a price.

JAMEY: Sorry.

PAUL: Most of us are still perfectly fine.

JAMEY: If I let your family escape, I won't get a good job like this again. This is steady work. It'd be easier without the nagging, but it's steady.

PAUL: Why are you doing this to us? We've never done anything to you.

JAMEY: Before this, I used to be a day laborer. You were merchants, right?

PAUL: We were shopkeepers.

JAMEY: Indoor work, steady. You had some security.

PAUL: A little.

JAMEY: Now I've got a little security. I like it. Back in the revolution, when Cromwell was running the place, I thought that might get me some security, but it didn't. The king came back, and I thought that might do it, but it didn't. Maybe the plague will do it.

PAUL: What kind of man profits from others' misfortune?

JAMEY: Well, there's doctors, ministers, nurses, grave-diggers. Merchants. What did you sell? Candles, wasn't it?

PAUL: Yes.

JAMEY: When I burn my last candle, and I'm sitting in the dark, that's a misfortune. And there you are, with a house full of candles, ready to sell me another one. So.

(On the lower level: MRS FINCH enters, carrying her white wand.)

FINCH: *(To PAUL)* Show me the body.

(The lights crossfade to:)

Scene Five

(On the lower level: LAWRENCE's *office.* LAWRENCE *seated,* HARMAN *pacing nervously.)*

HARMAN: I have changed my mind!

LAWRENCE: You've what?

HARMAN: I have changed my mind, that's all. Find someone else.

LAWRENCE: There is no one else. You're the best man I have.

HARMAN: Then God help you.

LAWRENCE: Well, he isn't. What do you want to do, Edward? Leave? Go to the country?

HARMAN: Most of my patients are in Salisbury with the Court.

LAWRENCE: They won't let you into Salisbury.

HARMAN: Why won't they?

LAWRENCE: You're here. They'll be afraid of you.

HARMAN: I knew it. I've stayed here too long as it is. I'll go into the country. Give me a pass.

LAWRENCE: But what would you do in the country?

HARMAN: I would fish.

LAWRENCE: The plague is spreading into the country. You'll only find yourself in another sickroom.

HARMAN: No, I would fish, and live in a village, write about what I've seen here, pass along what I've learned, I could write something very quickly and pass it to the College. They might listen to someone who was here.

LAWRENCE: But you want to leave. You want to be here and you want to leave. Which is it?

HARMAN: I have been here. I have done more than enough for a lifetime.

LAWRENCE: What do you imagine, you'll be welcomed by your colleagues? They'll either shun you, or persuade you to admit that what you've done here is pointless, and they were right to leave.

HARMAN: It is pointless! If I administer purgatives they die, if I don't administer purgatives they die, if I keep them warm they die, if I keep them cool they die, if I lance the buboes they die in terrible pain, and if I don't then they die of the pain from the buboes.

LAWRENCE: All of them?

HARMAN: They live or die no matter what I do. There's no pattern to it. I don't think I'm giving them anything.

LAWRENCE: What do they think?

HARMAN: They keep calling for me and calling for me....

LAWRENCE: So they think you're helping them.

HARMAN: And then they die.

LAWRENCE: Or not.

HARMAN: I didn't come here to argue with you, I came here to tell you my decision and get a pass to go. You owe me that.

LAWRENCE: I do, but—

HARMAN: We shouldn't even be arguing, anger is very bad, any excitation of the spirit encourages the disease, we are supposed to remain calm and unharried.

LAWRENCE: We are supposed to live in hope.

HARMAN: Funny, isn't it? Hope, yes.

LAWRENCE: Which appears to be what your patients are getting from you.

(Pause)

HARMAN: I've almost caught it, you know. Twice that I know of. Sweats, a few spots.

LAWRENCE: Yet here you are. Alive and well.

HARMAN: I'll die here.

LAWRENCE: No.

HARMAN: "No?" Say that again, "No?" You're such a politician, John, sitting there trying to win an argument. But do you have any idea what you're asking me to do?

LAWRENCE: No. If I knew what I'm asking, and it kept me from my duty, then many more people would die. So I can't know. Can I.

(CLERK enters.)

CLERK: My Lord? The constables have brought Reverend Vincent.

LAWRENCE: Show him in.

CLERK: And the constables?

LAWRENCE: No. Alone. Thank the constables and dismiss them.

CLERK: Doctor Harman, there's a surgeon's assistant waiting outside, he says you are wanted.

HARMAN: Naturally. How many patients?

CLERK: He said patient, sir. Singular, sir.

HARMAN: Well. If it's just one. I'll see one.

CLERK: Shall I—

HARMAN: No, I'll go myself.

(CLERK *exits.* HARMAN *moves to follow him.*)

LAWRENCE: Edward. This is a pass out of town. Take it.

HARMAN: God. The first thing I do I shall walk straight into a trout stream and stand in clear water up to here and catch my weight in trout and float them all free and then I shall walk to a village where scores of women are giving birth and pull every baby out alive and tie each one a beautiful navel and the only things I shall ever touch will be mothers and newborns and water and trout.

(CLERK *enters with* VINCENT.)

LAWRENCE: May I join you there someday?

HARMAN: Yes you may. (*He takes the pass from* LAWRENCE's *desk.*) Good luck, John.

(HARMAN *and* CLERK *exit.*)

VINCENT: Why have I been brought here?

LAWRENCE: Doctor Vincent. Do you know where you are?

VINCENT: London.

LAWRENCE: Do you know what you've done?

VINCENT: I have preached.

LAWRENCE: Do you know who I am?

VINCENT: You are the Lord Mayor.

LAWRENCE: I am the law here! It is against the law for you to be in London. It is against the law for you to preach. But you thought because the Court was gone, the law was gone as well. The penalty for what you've done is exile to the colonies.

VINCENT: With so many of my fellow dissenters? I returned to London in the midst of the plague. Do you seek to frighten me with a sea voyage?

LAWRENCE: Your fellows on the prison ships are dying like flies.

VINCENT: They are dying like martyrs.

LAWRENCE: Oh, is that why you've returned here?

VINCENT: I am here because I am needed here. The churches are open. The pulpits are empty.

LAWRENCE: And the law?

VINCENT: My parishioners tell me you are signing no more passes. You speak to me of principles and the law, while your friend the physician leaves with a pass in his hand.

(Pause)

LAWRENCE: Because he'll never use it.

VINCENT: You persuaded him not to leave?

LAWRENCE: He's better than that. He persuaded himself.

VINCENT: Perhaps you helped him to recall his better nature. Sir John, I think we may be doing similar work. Why do you help your friend to stay, and try to force me to go?

LAWRENCE: He is licensed. You are not.

VINCENT: Sir John, in my time I have been licensed and unlicensed and licensed with limits and unlicensed again. I have been arrested by monarchists, who are savage, I have been arrested by Puritans, who are savager still, and now I have been arrested by you. A businessman in a sash.

LAWRENCE: Do you know what I could do to you?

VINCENT: Sir John, I've been threatened by professionals. But I am not in prison, am I. I am not on the rack. I am not on a leaking ship to nowhere. I am not dead yet. I am in the office of the Lord Mayor of London. A man who is trying to run a city with no clergy.

LAWRENCE: I don't care to argue politics with you.

VINCENT: I don't care to argue religion. You're a practical man, Sir John. I'll wager you can't tell your good Anglican doctrine from my nonconformism, and I don't expect you care.

LAWRENCE: The people I answer to can tell the difference, and they care deeply.

VINCENT: And where are they? Dancing in Salisbury? We are here. The people of London are here. In their panic, will they think, because the churchmen have gone, that God has gone as well? Once they believe that, how ever will you govern them?

LAWRENCE: Doctor Vincent, I am not the only businessman in this room.

VINCENT: Sir John, for the moment, I am simply one denomination and you are another, like francs and sterling. Tell me the rate of exchange.

(Pause)

LAWRENCE: I can't use a traitor. I won't have treason preached here.

VINCENT: Have there been false reports of my preaching?

LAWRENCE: They tell me you've said God is punishing the kingdom.

VINCENT: Am I wrong?

LAWRENCE: You can't say it. Not if you're going to keep a pulpit.

(Pause)

VINCENT: Agreed.

LAWRENCE: Do you understand me?

VINCENT: Yes, sir.

LAWRENCE: Good. Good day, then.

VINCENT: Sir John, can you do nothing for my people on the prison ships?

LAWRENCE: It's not my jurisdiction.

VINCENT: Could you speak to the Duke of Albemarle?

LAWRENCE: Oh Lord.

VINCENT: If you tell him that my people are diseased? If you tell him they are suffering frightfully?

LAWRENCE: If I tell him that they might infect his Navy. That would do it.

VINCENT: Thank you, Sir John.

LAWRENCE: Don't thank me. Say you are in my debt.

(They look at each other. The lights crossfade to:)

Scene Six

(On the lower level: Lights up as SARAH enters, dressed for the road. She stops and looks around.)

ROBERT: *(Off)* Excuse me!

(ROBERT enters, opposite SARAH.)

SARAH: Good day, sir.

ROBERT: Good day.

SARAH: Is this the way to Walthamstow?

ROBERT: Walthamstow? I don't think so. No. Probably not.

SARAH: Are you walking toward London?

ROBERT: No, no, wouldn't want to do that.

SARAH: No.

ROBERT: Are you walking from London?

SARAH: I am returning to Oxford.

ROBERT: From London?

SARAH: That general area. The outskirts. Trading.

ROBERT: This isn't the road to Oxford.

SARAH: I was afraid of that. What's the next town up this road?

ROBERT: Well. Walthamstow.

SARAH: That's what I thought. Good, if I have to be lost I'm glad to know where I am. *(She smiles. Nothing from him.)* Are you traveling as well?

ROBERT: No, not really.

SARAH: You live here?

ROBERT: Yes, around about here.

SARAH: Good, well, so I continue up this road to Walthamstow.

ROBERT: No, I don't think so. Probably not.

SARAH: But—

(ANDREW and BILL enter.)

SARAH: Gentlemen. Good afternoon.

BILL: May we help you, ma'am.

SARAH: Thank you, I wish to find the road through Walthamstow.

BILL: From London?

SARAH: To Oxford.

BILL: Oxford isn't this way.

ROBERT: I explained all this to her, Bill.

BILL: You're so polite nobody can understand you. Ma'am, no one passes from the London way.

SARAH: I don't understand.

BILL: There's plague in London.

SARAH: Yes, I know.

BILL: We don't want it here.

SARAH: I can understand that.

BILL: So we have to keep the infected away.

SARAH: I am pleased to hear it, I have no wish to contact infected people. May I pass, please?

ROBERT: You've come from London.

SARAH: I have been near London.

BILL: Then you've been infected.

SARAH: No.

ROBERT: Close enough.

SARAH: What?

ROBERT: You probably have.

SARAH: I say I have not.

BILL: A lot have said that. Now they're dead.

SARAH: Gentlemen, I agree with you. I want to live among healthy people. I am a healthy person. I can prove I am. And I—

ANDREW: You can prove that you're healthy.

SARAH: Thank you, sir, yes, I can. *(She rummages in her bag.)*

BILL: But Andrew—

ANDREW: You have a certificate declaring that you are healthy?

SARAH: Yes I do, I have it right here. *(She pulls it from her bag and holds it out.)*

ANDREW: Those are issued only to citizens of London. *(Pause)* You are a citizen of London, then. *(Pause)* My friends could have saved you time. People who have visited London for trade may pass through the fields. Londoners we turn back.

SARAH: Infected Londoners, of course, I understand. I'm sorry, I should have explained better, I am a good woman and not used to bargaining with men in the road as you force me to.

BILL: Not our choice.

ANDREW: And we're not bargaining. We're turning you back.

SARAH: Gentlemen, I have a certificate of health, signed by a surgeon from the College of Physicians.

ANDREW: We used to trust people with certificates, and let them through. One died in our inn, of the plague. We don't trust them anymore.

SARAH: Have some good woman examine my body for sores.

ANDREW: We've heard there's time between catching it and showing it. Why do you try to fool us with that?

BILL: There's no point arguing. The rule is made.

ANDREW: I'm explaining to her. Ma'am, this town and London, we've done good business.

SARAH: Yes, we have, I have traveled this road, gentlemen, helping in my husband's trade, I know this town, this is a good town.

ANDREW: Where's your husband now? Dead of the plague?

SARAH: Spotted fever.

ANDREW: And your children?

SARAH: My children are well.

ANDREW: In London?

SARAH: Gentlemen, please.

ANDREW: I thought as much.

BILL: Stand where you are.

ROBERT: Go back now.

ANDREW: Ma'am, we have nothing against Londoners here. Do you understand? Further up this road you'd hear talk about the sins of the city. You'd hear about comeuppance. We're not saying that. We are protecting ourselves. Once this plague is done, we want no talk in London of unfairness from here. And the next time you come, we hope to trade again.

SARAH: Please believe me, I am well.

ANDREW: You don't know, yourself. You could be standing there now, infected.

SARAH: Quarantine me. Here, by this road. I have a little money, some, enough for some food, and with your charity I can prove—

BILL: Here? Upwind of the town? Andrew, some of them say the contagion comes on the wind.

ANDREW: I'm sorry. Not here.

SARAH: Let me pass through the fields.

ANDREW: If we let Londoners through our fields, the next towns north will suspect us of infection. They'll cut us off.

BILL: We have a responsibility.

SARAH: I won't turn around here and walk back to my death, I won't do it.

BILL: You have to.

SARAH: I have to pass.

BILL: We have to stop you.

SARAH: Try!

(Pause ROBERT *runs off.)*

SARAH: If I am infected, you wouldn't want to lay hands on me. Much better for me to pass right through your town. I'll pass through, I'll touch nothing, I'll breathe shallowly. If you try to stop me, I will throw myself into your arms. I am a good woman, I have never spoken in this way, I'm sorry.

(ROBERT *reenters. He is carrying a musket.)*

ROBERT: Ma'am? This is a musket. We will use it.

BILL: If you were a good woman, you wouldn't have brought us to this.

SARAH: Have you shot other Londoners? Where are they? Do you roll them into a ditch, what?

ROBERT: We have not.

BILL: We could.

ROBERT: Others have. In other towns.

ANDREW: Some places they've sat down in the road, like you. They've begged and starved. And gotten no explanation.

SARAH: I am not a beggar, I have never been a beggar, I have had a house and a family, we had a trade. I have children. I have three children. You don't know my name. We might be standing here a while, and you should know who I am. My name is Sarah Chandler. You see? We're alike.

ANDREW: No. Not right now. Before, and later, but not now. You have to go.

SARAH: No. I don't have to. I can stand here.

ROBERT: We'll shoot.

SARAH: All right, then.

(Pause)

ANDREW: Don't make us do this.

(SARAH *takes a step toward them.)*

SARAH: My husband. George. He'd have protected me. He'd have done what you're doing. He was just like you.

(SARAH *takes another step.* BILL *steps back a pace. The others do not.* SARAH *peers at* ROBERT, *who glances away.*)

ANDREW: Bill. Go get the dogs.

(BILL *exits.*)

ANDREW: I'm sorry, ma'am. You leave us no choice.

SARAH: No, that's all right. This road's no good to me now.

ANDREW: Thank you.

SARAH: I'm trying to get away from infection. (*She begins pacing backward, deliberately.*)

ANDREW: What are you saying? There's no infection here.

SARAH: No? Have you ever seen plague tokens? I have. (*She points at* ROBERT.) Look at him. You see that place on his neck?

ROBERT: There's nothing on my neck.

ANDREW: Of course not.

SARAH: You know best, I'm sure. Good day, gentlemen. (*She turns on her heel and exits.*)

ROBERT: We could shoot you if we wanted to! Calls herself a good woman. There's nothing on my neck.

ANDREW: Of course not.

(BILL *enters at a run.*)

BILL: There they go!

ROBERT: Scolding like a fishwife.

(*Pause*)

ANDREW: There is, though, actually. Just a little.

(ROBERT *tries to see his neck, and feels it.*)

ROBERT: What? That? Scar from a goiter, had it for years. I have.

ANDREW: Yes, of course.

BILL: What's going on?

ROBERT: It's true.

(*As they go, the lights crossfade to:*)

Scene Seven

(On the lower level: GRAUNT *enters and watches as:)*

(On the upper level: HARMAN *enters, in his protective suit. He removes it piece by piece, slowly, as if at the end of a long and exhausting day. First the head piece, then the gloves, then the cloak, then the boots. During this,* GRAUNT *turns and speaks:)*

GRAUNT: There came a time for each of us. Mine came the first time I ran a fever. When I realized I was ill, and what it might be, the sweat burst out of me. I knew it was probably nothing, but I sent for the doctor and I took to my bed and I waited to learn if I was dying. Terribly frightened. Hadn't expected that. Worth noting. I dozed, finally, and fell into a sleep. In my fever I was vouchsafed a dream.

*(*HARMAN's *black clothing is piled at his feet by now, and he is dressed in a light shirt and trousers. During the following, he removes his shirt and examines his chest.)*

GRAUNT: I dreamed I was dying, there in my room. And a figure came to me, of a tall man, young, dressed all in linen. And I said to him, "Are you the Angel of Death?" And he said— I'll never forget— he said, "No, I asked to fetch you myself. I am the Recording Angel. Your desk is waiting. Come and help me to number the hosts of heaven."

*(*HARMAN *finds something under his arm.)*

HARMAN: Oh, Jesus. *(He frantically searches his other side.)*

GRAUNT: I woke up smiling. But I had learned. I was here.

*(*HARMAN *finds the same thing under his other arm. He feels his throat.)*

HARMAN: Oh, Jesus. Oh, Jesus.

(The lights fade quickly.)

END OF ACT ONE

ACT TWO

Scene One

(An empty stage. On the lower level: SARAH *enters, trudging, and crosses to her spot on the steps.)*

SARAH: Anybody home? *(Pause)* Mary? Paul? *(Pause)* Chris? Becca? Georgie? *(Pause)* Anybody home? *(She curls up on the steps.)*

(On the lower level: GRAUNT *enters.)*

GRAUNT: People ask me what the plague looked like. It looks like this. You wander through a crowd of absences. Friends gone, of course, but more than that. The plague is a place where you search for strangers. Where are the crowds? I don't know where I'm going without the crowds. They were my landmarks. The crowds in the morning, that was the Exchange. The crowds at noon, that was Westminster. The people milling about in the evening, that was Drury Lane. They told me I was somewhere. Where am I now?

A long, open space. It used to be a street, but there's nowhere to go, and no one passes, so what is it now? A narrow meadow, where cinders bloom. All around it stand great wooden crates. They had doors and windows once, but those are nailed shut, crosses painted on them. They are crates full of poisoned air, standing in the air. You say, I don't know this place, I have to get out of here. I'll go to the fields. I'll stand in the crowds of grain, and I'll know where I am.

But when you walk to where the fields should be, the grain is gone. New hills are there, and new valleys. And this is where the crowds have gone. The surface of the earth can't hold them all and the pits are full to bursting. The people are becoming the land, and the land has broken out in sores.

I wandered around the edge of that place, where London went into the ground. I have always gone where the crowds have gone. To be alive, in this place, feels somehow like a rude mistake. Something that just isn't done anymore.

So as you walk, if you spot another living person, any other person in the world, your heart stands up, and dances. You want to run to that person, hold your heart against theirs, so your hearts can dance together. But you mustn't, you mustn't touch them, you mustn't come close to them. So you wave wildly and call out, as if you were two little boats on the high sea of the plague, unable to approach for fear the waves would crash the two of you together and you would crush each other. And this is London now: a dry sea, laced with narrow channels, hemmed in by wooden rocks full of poisoned air, where you row the little boat of your body. And now and then you see a sail on the horizon, and you wave, and it waves back, and then you take up your oars again, rowing and rowing through the ashes.

(GRAUNT *exits as the lights crossfade to:*)

(*On the lower level:* LAWRENCE *enters. He sees* SARAH, *and crosses to sit on the steps at a distance from her. He rests for a little while. She becomes aware of him and sits up, slowly.*)

LAWRENCE: What are you doing?

(*Pause*)

SARAH: This used to be my house.

LAWRENCE: What are you doing here now?

SARAH: This used to be my yard.

(*Pause*)

LAWRENCE: What are you doing?

SARAH: I can sit in my own yard if I want to. Why are you asking a lot of questions?

LAWRENCE: I'm supposed to be minding things around here.

SARAH: Hell of a job you're doing.

LAWRENCE: Could be worse.

SARAH: You think so? You've got quite an imagination.

(*Pause*)

LAWRENCE: You've lost family?

SARAH: No, I know where they are.

LAWRENCE: What are you doing here?

SARAH: Going to join them.

LAWRENCE: By sitting here?

SARAH: All you have to do is sit still and it comes to pick you up.

LAWRENCE: What does? Hackney coach?

SARAH: Death cart.

LAWRENCE: Do you feel ill? Should I get you a doctor?

SARAH: I'm all right. I was just sitting here till you came up and wanted my travel plans.

(*Pause*)

LAWRENCE: So you're sitting here.

SARAH: You *must* be the one in charge of this, it makes sense now.

LAWRENCE: You must be a shopkeeper's wife.

SARAH: Shopkeeper's widow.

LAWRENCE: Thought so. I'm married to one myself. Tongue like a razor. (*Pause*) My wife, remarkable, I've bought her a certain leisure, house full of servants. Me, I can sit for hours. She's got no knack for it. Just like you, I expect. She walks around, wipes this up, mends that, checks the accounts payable one more time. She's also given me a great many daughters, so she always has negotiating to do. They're in the country now.

SARAH: Lucky them.

(*Pause*)

LAWRENCE: I expect you're used to being useful. Come on.

SARAH: Where?

LAWRENCE: Anywhere. Lots to do.

SARAH: My house is closed. Our shop is shut. My family's dead. My work is all done.

LAWRENCE: Big house, London. Big shop. I used to sit in meetings, now there's no people to meet with so I walk around. I walk around London like a housewife now, saying, "What else needs doing? There must be something else to do." And there always is. Interesting way to live.

(LAWRENCE *stands and takes some scraps of paper from his wallet. He shuffles through them, takes one and lays it on the ground between himself and* SARAH.)

LAWRENCE: So. Go here first.

(SARAH *looks at the piece of paper.*)

SARAH: I've got my ride coming.

LAWRENCE: Go here first. Two streets down, turn left, third house. There's a woman sick, in childbed. She won't survive, neither will the baby.

SARAH: What do you want me to do about it?

LAWRENCE: Everything you can. I expect that's a lot.

SARAH: No.

LAWRENCE: I expect it's more than you know. Now. Doctor Harman will be coming to check on them this afternoon. Tell him I sent you. After they're dead, report to him. There's food and a bit of money. Enough to keep body and soul together.

SARAH: Mine aren't on the best of terms.

LAWRENCE: Comes of sitting still. There's the address.

(LAWRENCE *exits.* SARAH *looks at the piece of paper as the lights crossfade to:*)

Scene Two

(*On the lower level: Lights up as* LAWRENCE'S CLERK *enters, carrying a set of tongs with very long handles and a large leather portfolio.* BROUNKER'S CLERK *enters, carrying a flaming brazier of coals, which he sets between them.*)

LAWRENCE'S CLERK: Morning.

BROUNKER'S CLERK: Morning. How's London?

LAWRENCE'S CLERK: Worse. Tim Bishop died.

BROUNKER'S CLERK: I liked him.

(BROUNKER'S CLERK *exits.* LAWRENCE'S CLERK *looks back over his shoulder and checks quickly in his portfolio.* BROUNKER'S CLERK *reenters carrying his own set of long-handled tongs and portfolio.*)

BROUNKER'S CLERK: Yours coming?

LAWRENCE'S CLERK: Yeah. Yours waiting?

BROUNKER'S CLERK: Yeah.

LAWRENCE'S CLERK: Shit.

(GRAUNT *enters hurriedly, carrying a large sheaf of papers.*)

GRAUNT: Is this the place?

LAWRENCE'S CLERK: Yes, sir. Have you seen him?

GRAUNT: No, haven't you?

LAWRENCE'S CLERK: Look sharp.

(LORD BROUNKER *enters. Everyone bows.*)

BROUNKER: Do you have the Bill of Mortality?

LAWRENCE'S CLERK: Yes, my Lord.

BROUNKER: I shall examine it.

LAWRENCE'S CLERK: My Lord, I expect he'll be along in a very few moments. (*During the following, he takes a large sheet of paper from his portfolio, lays it carefully on the ground, and picks it up with his set of tongs.*) He is often out of the office, my Lord, and the bells ring so often for the d...for so many things. It is difficult to tell the time.

GRAUNT: Lord Brounker, it is good to see you again. Graunt—

BROUNKER: Mr Graunt, yes—

GRAUNT: John Graunt, we have met, if you— when I was accepted into the Royal Society?

BROUNKER: Ah, yes.

GRAUNT: And then again, it would have been a year ago, no, November last, and here it is only July, is it only eight months, how slowly the year is going. Eight months ago—

BROUNKER: At a Royal Society meeting.

GRAUNT: How kind of you to remember, yes, the session at which Mr Clarke and Mr Pearse fed opium to the greyhound.

BROUNKER: Most informative, yes.

(*During this exchange,* LAWRENCE'S CLERK, *using his tongs, holds the piece of paper out to* BROUNKER'S CLERK, *who receives it in his set of tongs and holds it in the smoke of the brazier before holding it out to* BROUNKER, *who takes it and examines it.*)

GRAUNT: Sir John asked me to come along today to present some observations I have made with regard to the Bills of Mortality, that is the most recent—

BROUNKER: This is frightful.

GRAUNT: Yes. But its true significance is only revealed in relation to the others, which I—

(LAWRENCE *enters, a bit winded.*)

LAWRENCE: Good day, my Lord. Did I keep you waiting?

BROUNKER: Good day, Sir John. I was not waiting.

LAWRENCE: The Court's move from Salisbury to Oxford went smoothly?

BROUNKER: Thank you, yes. There was some concern over Lady Castlemayne, who is very near her time to be traveling, but all went bravely.

LAWRENCE: London salutes them. The King is well?

BROUNKER: Quite well. (*Pause*) It is good to see you looking so well.

LAWRENCE: I *am* well.

BROUNKER: That is good. I have examined the Bill of Mortality for the week. Your losses are frightful.

LAWRENCE: Yes, they are. As I have asked Mr Graunt here to explain. Have you met?

BROUNKER: Yes, we've known each other quite some time.

LAWRENCE: Graunt?

(GRAUNT *kneels and spreads out his sheets of paper on the ground as he speaks.*)

GRAUNT: As you can see, the plague is flowing eastward.

BROUNKER: Yes.

GRAUNT: Parishes close to the center of London are reporting many more cases than last week, and even the most eastern suburbs now have a few.

BROUNKER: But the west is improving. The cases are fewer.

GRAUNT: So are the people. You can see that all deaths are fewer there, from all causes, but higher in the east. The people are moving eastward, taking the plague along with them.

BROUNKER: Can they be stopped?

GRAUNT: They should have been, yes, by taking care of them where they were. Look at the pattern. The losses were always worst in the most overcrowded districts.

BROUNKER: Yes...

GRAUNT: Now we see that pattern, the exact pattern, duplicated in districts that once had light and space and air. The people ran away to healthy neighborhoods and crowded into them and now they bear the same numbers as the most teeming slums. Do you see? The number of losses is rising, and not only the number of losses, but the speed at which the losses rise, and not only the speed at which they rise, but the speed at which the rise is rising. The rate of acceleration, you see?

BROUNKER: Ah, yes.

GRAUNT: Do you see?

BROUNKER: You may have lost me toward the end there.

GRAUNT: Look at the Bills! Turn the pages week by week, you see a great wave of numbers sweeping across London, spilling here, eddying there, stagnating and deepening—

LAWRENCE: Thank you, Mr Graunt.

GRAUNT: *(On his knees among his papers)* It's all here. Anyone can see it.

BROUNKER: Most informative. *(He nods and turns away.)*

GRAUNT: It's all...right here.

BROUNKER: Sir John, are the regulations being enforced?

LAWRENCE: Insofar as we are able. Enforcement requires healthy enforcers, and there are very few of them left. Especially given the wages.

BROUNKER: Is the nation's charity not sufficient?

LAWRENCE: They give little, which lengthens the emergency, so they give even less. We had hoped the Court might respond.

BROUNKER: We have done so.

(BROUNKER'S CLERK *takes a large piece of vellum from his portfolio and, using his tongs, passes it to* LAWRENCE'S CLERK, *who takes it in his tongs and passes it to* LAWRENCE, *who stares at it, during the following.*)

BROUNKER: The King has proclaimed a monthly fast day on which collections will be taken at churches across the country. There is the list of subscribers. You'll see his majesty's signature, encouragingly large.

LAWRENCE: But the Privy Council sends no money.

BROUNKER: The Council has the defense of the nation to consider. According to our intelligence reports, the Dutch believe we are powerless in the grip of this disease and are preparing what they hope will be a death blow against our shipping. What about the Poor Rate?

LAWRENCE: We have great trouble collecting the Poor Rate from the landholders, because they have abandoned the city. Even if we could it would be too little.

GRAUNT: Half the remaining households are infected.

LAWRENCE: My supply lines for food are down to a trickle.

BROUNKER: Sir John—

LAWRENCE: There are almost no pest houses, those are full, and so dangerous that many would rather die alone than be taken there. We need more death carts, more sea coal for fires to purge the air, new graves must be dug, the laystalls are polluting the drinking water, garbage rots in the streets—

BROUNKER: Jack. There is not enough money in the entire Exchequer to supply all of these.

LAWRENCE: Supply *one.* Any *one.*

BROUNKER: These needs are desperate, but this is a desperate time. You knew it would be so as well as we. All you pledged was to keep the situation in control. Are you reporting that the situation is out of your control?

LAWRENCE: No, I am not reporting that, but—

BROUNKER: I ask merely because you seem, perhaps, overscheduled.

LAWRENCE: I am certainly undermanned.

(Pause)

BROUNKER: The city is lacking certain essentials. I will make this known.

(BROUNKER crosses up the steps to the upper level. LAWRENCE pursues him.)

LAWRENCE: No one will trade with us. No one will allow us to leave the city. Whole areas of the Isles— all of Scotland forbids any Londoner even to cross the border. We are pariahs in our own country. How are we to live?

BROUNKER: I will make this known. I will make all of this known.

LAWRENCE: It is known. Everyone knows our trouble, that is why we are shunned. Make it felt.

(The lights crossfade to:)

Scene Three

(On the lower level: FINCH is sprawled on the floor at a distance from the cot. She tries to put weight on her legs. She moans, and stops. She wipes her face on her shoulder.)

FINCH: Stupid cow. Try the arms. *(She tries putting weight on her arms and yells at the pain.)* Jesus *Christ*! Better. Off we go. *(Balling her fists, she plants them on the floor ahead of her. She takes a deep breath and pulls herself forward. She breathes for a moment, then pulls herself forward. Then she loses her nerve and sinks back.)* All right, Lizabeth. Doctor sees you can't walk, you're a goner. *(She gathers herself.)* Bet you can't get into bed before he comes. *(She hauls herself forward three times.)* Jesus Christ Jesus *Christ* Jesus *Christ*! *(She collapses, panting.)* I am not cursing. I am praying. *(She gets up on her fists again.)* Elizabeth Finch. You can do this. Three more steps. *(She shuts her eyes and pulls herself forward.)* Come on, Lizabeth. Two more. *(She pulls herself forward.)* Poor little Lizzie. One more step to Mama.

(She pulls herself forward and opens her eyes. She is a few feet shy of the bed. She reaches out and touches the frame, a long stretch away. She leans her head on her arm and cries.)

SARAH: *(Off)* Is anyone up there!

(FINCH looks up, fearful.)

FINCH: *(In a hoarse whisper)* Here.

SARAH: *(Off)* Is anyone up there!

(FINCH *grabs the edge of the bed with both hands. Too quickly to change her mind, she drags herself into the bed.*)

FINCH: Yaaaah! (*She sits in the bed, her breathing ragged and deep.*) I win.

(SARAH *enters, carrying a bag.*)

FINCH: Sarah. Well, now. Good of you to call.

SARAH: Mrs Finch. You're ill.

FINCH: Been better, been better. When you called, I thought you were a nurse down there. Doctor's coming any moment, you see, so I don't know how long I'll be able to—

SARAH: He'll be along.

(SARAH *pulls a set of leather straps from the bag and tosses them to* FINCH. *Each strap has a loop at one end.*)

SARAH: Wrists and ankles.

FINCH: You're the nurse?

(SARAH *takes a pair of gloves from the bag and sets them aside.*)

FINCH: Since when?

SARAH: Days now. Wrists and ankles.

(FINCH *loosely straps one ankle to the frame of the cot.* SARAH *pulls a kerchief and a small bottle of spirits from the bag. During the following, she soaks the cloth in the spirits.*)

FINCH: I was sorry to hear about your family.

(SARAH *looks at her.*)

FINCH: I wish I could have done even more to help.

SARAH: Other ankle.

FINCH: I, ah...the sores.

SARAH: Where.

(FINCH *points to her groin, both sides.*)

SARAH: Just around the ankle, then.

(FINCH *puts the strap around the other ankle and lets the loose end dangle.* SARAH *ties the cloth over her own mouth and nose and puts the gloves on.*)

FINCH: Do you know who's been doing my job the last few days? Must be a hell of a backlog. Have you— seen a lot of cases?

(SARAH *crosses to kneel next to* FINCH *without ever touching her.* FINCH *hesitates, then puts her wrists in the loops of the straps.*)

SARAH: Arms to your sides.

(FINCH *does so, and* SARAH *winds the strap of one wrist around the bed frame and ties it.*)

FINCH: Sarah?

(SARAH *silences her with a look. As* FINCH *watches,* SARAH *crosses to the other side and does the same to the other wrist.*)

FINCH: I know you, Sarah. You're a good girl.

(FINCH *is leaning up on her elbows.* SARAH *kneels next to the unbound ankle.*)

FINCH: Sarah. The children barely suffered at all.

(SARAH *looks at* FINCH *expressionlessly, takes the dangling end of the strap and winds it once around the bed frame.*)

FINCH: They went in their sleep. All of them. They looked so peaceful.

(*They look at each other.* SARAH *pulls the strap tight, forcing* FINCH's *legs apart.* FINCH *chokes back a scream. They stay like that for a long moment.*)

HARMAN: *(Off)* Elizabeth Finch?

FINCH: Eeyyesss!

(SARAH *stands as* HARMAN *enters, carrying his headpiece.* VINCENT *follows him.*)

HARMAN: Running late. How is she?

FINCH: Get her out of here!

SARAH: Delirious.

FINCH: You—!

HARMAN: Buboes?

SARAH: In the groin.

HARMAN: Ah huh... (HARMAN *puts on his headpiece and prepares to examine her.*)

FINCH: Wait! No!

HARMAN: Lie still.

(HARMAN *bends over* FINCH *and begins his examination. She cannot help but gasp in pain. He straightens up.*)

HARMAN: I thought as much.

FINCH: *(To* VINCENT*)* You! Please! Give me something.

VINCENT: I am not the physician.

FINCH: *(To* HARMAN*)* I don't want you yet! *(To* VINCENT*)* You, the minister.

(HARMAN *moves to go.*)

HARMAN: Fine. I have too many other patients.

VINCENT: *(To* HARMAN*)* Where are you going?

HARMAN: If she thinks I can't help her, I can't do a thing. My other patients don't know I can't help them, so I might be able to fool them into getting well.

(FINCH *moans.*)

VINCENT: You can't leave her.

HARMAN: The buboes in her groin have hardened and are eating into her vitals. Unless I lance them, the pain will continue until she dies.

FINCH: No! He wants to spade it out of me!

HARMAN: She knows, you see. If I lance them, I may kill her with the pain.

VINCENT: Stay a few minutes.

HARMAN: The nurse will stay.

FINCH: No! Not the nurse!

VINCENT: You have to do something, you're here to do something, so do it! Otherwise why are you here?

HARMAN: I don't know! Why are you? *(Pause. To* SARAH:*)* Prepare the instruments, Mrs Chandler.

(SARAH *lays out several horrific devices during the following.*)

FINCH: *(To* VINCENT*)* Give me something!

HARMAN: *(To* VINCENT*)* Go ahead. Show me how it's done.

VINCENT: How may I help you, good woman?

FINCH: Give me something.

VINCENT: What?

FINCH: Blessing, penance, absolution, something. I've been a sinner, led into sin, this one here for one—

SARAH: Me?

VINCENT: This woman wishes you to recover.

FINCH: No! They've tempted me with bribes, they used my need, the parish, the aldermen—

VINCENT: The parish led you into sin?

FINCH: They hire sinners, anyone with a job like mine, they think our souls are damned already, but they're wrong, aren't they?

VINCENT: Of course they are. It is good your trial leads you to these thoughts.

FINCH: I repent my yielding to their temptations.

VINCENT: Then you shall be saved.

FINCH: Bless you, bless you—

VINCENT: For your salvation to be complete, you must forgive her.

(Pause)

FINCH: Sarah? *(Spat like a curse)* Forgive you.

SARAH: *(A curse back)* Forgive you, too.

HARMAN: Shall we begin?

FINCH: *(To* VINCENT*)* Have you done it? My salvation.

VINCENT: Yes.

FINCH: All right. As long as that's fixed up.

VINCENT: God keep you all, then.

HARMAN: Where are you going?

VINCENT: I have many other parishioners to see.

HARMAN: Last rites may be called for, save yourself a trip. Unless you feel they're unnecessary, after such a deeply convincing repentance.

(Pause)

VINCENT: We do what we can with what we're given. God has to know that. He is not an idiot.

SARAH: *(Very quietly, to no one)* Why's He doing this, then.

*(*HARMAN *takes an instrument and bends over* FINCH.*)*

HARMAN: Would you pray for me, too? I don't feel well at all.

*(*FINCH *screams bloody murder.)*

(The lights crossfade to:)

Scene Four

(On the upper level: Lights up on GRAUNT.*)*

GRAUNT: And here, I confess it, there is a gap in my account.

People ask me, "Did you...lose anyone? Did anyone close to you..." Die, is what they mean. And that question, that question...is not their fault. They weren't there, you see. As I was. They're not...here. Always.

Did you lose anyone. Who died.

In the month of June, we lost a thousand people to the plague. In the month of July, we lost a thousand people every week. In the month of August, we lost a thousand people every day. And one day, after all the deaths that had gone before, and with everyone gone from the city who could, with so few of us left alive, one day, toward summer's end, we lost a thousand every hour.

You have to understand: We did not know this at the time. All we knew... all we knew was that the sun was very hot. From dawn onwards it was a noontime sun, at a steeper and steeper angle, unblinking, until it stood in the center of the sky and that was all we knew, that the sun was very hot, and there was nowhere we could go and not hear screaming.

I say we lost a thousand every hour, but it was probably more, for that day...that was the day we lost count of ourselves. And what we did, what we must have done to be among those still alive by the end of that day, none of us can tell. We became a different species, without the power to speak to you. And then we were human again, but with no words for what we must have done.

On that day, everyone in London died. All of us.

Some of us...came back.

But with a gap in our accounts.

But this must be part of what I tell you, as your guide to this place, like our cartographers, who, in the places of which no description is possible, can only write: "Here There Be Tygers."

(The lights crossfade to:)

Scene Five

(On the lower level: HARMAN *and* SARAH *enter, he in his protective suit, she carrying the bag of gear.* SARAH *gets a quizzical look on her face, and stops.* HARMAN *notices she is no longer beside him, and turns. Her eyes are shut, and she is smiling.)*

HARMAN: Mrs Chandler?

SARAH: Oh, that's lovely.

HARMAN: Mrs Chandler. Are you well.

(She opens her eyes and points at his headpiece.)

SARAH: Oh, take that thing off.

(He pulls off the headpiece.)

HARMAN: I had forgotten I had it on, if you can— Oh. A breeze. Oh my—

SARAH: Mm.

HARMAN: When was the last time I felt the air moving.

(SARAH opens her hands in the breeze and chortles with helpless pleasure. HARMAN takes off his gloves.)

HARMAN: God knows where it's been.

SARAH: I do not care.

(HARMAN sniffs the air, first tentatively, then deeply.)

HARMAN: What is that.... Straw?

SARAH: Fresher. Hay.

HARMAN: New-mown hay.

SARAH: Somewhere someone is mowing hay.

HARMAN: A man with a scythe.

SARAH: What does it—

HARMAN: —remind you of?

(They breathe the air hungrily.)

SARAH: I'm getting a bit light-headed.

HARMAN: Be careful.

SARAH: Funny. I've lived in London my whole life, and never been here.

HARMAN: This district?

SARAH: The middle of the street. Only at a run, looking out for carriages. Worth your life to stand this long, before. Feels a bit wicked. If this ever ends, and I survive, I should like to stand perfectly still for a very long time.

HARMAN: It's dying down.

SARAH: Come back! Come— !

(The breeze picks up again. They smile.)

HARMAN: Ha! Well done!

(SARAH shuts her eyes and bathes her arms in the wind. HARMAN looks around him, and down.)

HARMAN: This was one of the busiest streets in London. Look at it. Grass is growing.

SARAH: Who does it remind me of...oh....

(*Her voice trails away, and she breathes in the scent of the air. She chuckles, quiet and deep. She opens her eyes.* HARMAN *is staring at her. He glances away and she looks down. Pause.*)

HARMAN: There it goes.

SARAH: There it goes.

HARMAN: Mrs Chandler, I— there's something I would like to ask you, but—well, it is awkward.

SARAH: Please.

HARMAN: Well, as you may have noticed, I have not been as strong in the last few days as I have been, and with that and some other signs, I think it is clear that I am...not well.

SARAH: I'm sorry.

HARMAN: It is probably a mild case, really, and I have survived before, it is probably nothing very much, really, just a quite minor case of the bubonic plague. (*He hears what he's said, and bursts out laughing.*) When I think of the things I used to worry about.

SARAH: You wanted to ask me something.

HARMAN: I've seen what happens to people...later in this. Many become delirious. Some run into the street. In their fever they can infect others.

SARAH: I've never seen that happen.

HARMAN: None of my patients has, because we bind them firmly. But I've seen them struggle.

SARAH: Perhaps they just don't want to be tied up.

HARMAN: Of course not, but they have to be. I'm afraid that when the fever comes upon me, I might escape. I can't have that. I've worked very hard against this disease, and I won't be responsible for spreading it. I'm afraid of what I might do, when I'm not in my right mind.

SARAH: You want me to bind you to a bed?

HARMAN: Yes, but I'm stronger than you, so that may not hold me. Now listen to me please. I know that sometimes you nurses will wait until a patient is asleep, loot his valuables, and abandon him to die alone.

SARAH: I never.

HARMAN: I've heard you do.

SARAH: Me?

HARMAN: Nurses in general.

SARAH: Have you seen this?

HARMAN: I've heard it said, by gentlemen whose word I trust.

SARAH: Of course, then, you know best.

HARMAN: Now. I have an arrangement to suggest. I shall tell you, before I die, an inventory of my most valuable possessions. Some you would not recognize nor know where to find without my help. I shall relate these to you in order of increasing value. It will be well worth your time. In exchange you will stay by me, and watch for signs that I am no longer myself. Now. I also know that you nurses will sometimes grow tired of waiting and smother your patients.

SARAH: I—

HARMAN: I say I have heard many stories of this. When I begin to struggle, I want you to smother me. I gather you know how to do it in such a way that there is little danger of detection. Two wet cloths, one laid over the other, covering my mouth and nose. And sit upon my chest if that seems called for.

SARAH: You medical men have a very low opinion of nurses.

HARMAN: Mrs Chandler. I am not blaming you. It's wrong, but the times are wrong, and if we are to survive we must act as the times permit. Do you agree?

SARAH: I have not been nursing long, sir. Perhaps a more experienced nurse would be more skilled at this operation.

HARMAN: There are very few nurses left alive. By the time you find one, it may be too late. Listen. With what I'll give you, you won't have to nurse anymore to survive. You are alone in the world. A widow.

SARAH: Yes, Sir.

HARMAN: In a desperate city, with no support, nothing for comfort? What else could you have done?

SARAH: When my husband was alive, I used an accurate scale. I kept true accounts. From the hour of his death I've been treated like a thief.

HARMAN: Mrs Chandler, I—

SARAH: They wouldn't even let me out of London, I think they would have shot me, but I said, if you think I have the plague and you shoot me, then what will you do? I'll still have the plague, but I'll be dead in the middle of your road.

HARMAN: Good for you.

SARAH: So they set the dogs on me. I ran down the road with the dogs snapping at me until they called them back. Then they whipped the dogs into the ditch and shot them.

HARMAN: Why?

SARAH: They had touched me, the dogs. I heard one of the men crying. One of the dogs must have been a favorite of his. I'm standing in the road a quarter mile back toward London and I can hear the man crying over his dog. And all for nothing, I wasn't sick, I told them I wasn't—

HARMAN: Where was this?

SARAH: Walthamstow, a month ago.

HARMAN: The plague is in Walthamstow now.

SARAH: Good!

(He looks at her. She turns away. Long pause.)

HARMAN: You came back here and nursed the sick. Why?

SARAH: I was hungry.

HARMAN: It was brave and good of you.

SARAH: I was a shopkeeper's wife, sick people are the only commodity now.

HARMAN: It was good of you.

(Pause)

SARAH: Most of the doctors left long ago. Why did you stay?

HARMAN: I had no choice either.

SARAH: Why not?

HARMAN: I have my own dogs, to set on myself. *(He touches his head.)* I kennel them here. *(He starts to walk again.)* We should be on our way. Where's the next patient?

SARAH: Are you sure you want me to do what you asked?

HARMAN: Yes. Will you do it?

SARAH: I'll stay with you.

HARMAN: And the other?

(The lights crossfade to:)

Scene Six

(On the lower level: GRAUNT *and* LAWRENCE *enter, in conversation.)*

GRAUNT: I was visiting the offices of Cripplegate parish, I wanted to check on what I suspected was some terrible underreporting. The office was locked, in the middle of the day, I called, no answer, I found a sexton, we broke in, and there was the parish clerk, at his desk, parish register on his desk, his head on the parish register.

LAWRENCE: Dead? Of the plague.

GRAUNT: In the middle of making an entry. I told the sexton to go for a doctor, he said the man was dead, we needed a searcher, I ordered him to go for a doctor, I was very upset, I didn't know why, I hadn't known the man. The sexton went for help, and I stood there, looking. I should have left the room, but I couldn't help looking.

LAWRENCE: At a corpse? You must have had your fill of—

GRAUNT: At the ledger. He'd been underreporting, and now I understood why, he must have been ill, so I wanted to see his numbers. I could see on the open page, almost the last thing he'd written. I was peering around his head. There was ink on his cheek. The entry for plague read 504.

LAWRENCE: My God. For one parish? For one week?

GRAUNT: I stood there thinking, 504. Yes, terrible. But. Did he count himself?

LAWRENCE: Graunt.

GRAUNT: I stood there, thinking that. May I tell you something? You have been so open to my information.

LAWRENCE: It has been of help. It will be in the future as well.

GRAUNT: Yes, so I think it's important that you know this. You see, I have always followed the trends. And death is so much the rage now. Sometimes the plague so infects my mind that I begin to think, all right, perhaps the world would not be worse off, with fewer people. Not excluding myself in this, not by any means. Each of us is a loose end, really. I know what a sinful thought this is. I put it down quickly. But the thought returns. I think of the world as a great equation, a problem whose solution I pursue with too much impatience. So many wretched sufferers, and their suffering children, on and on. Whole groups of people would simplify matters considerably if they would just disappear. I think this! And then I remember how I yearn for people who think like me to govern the world. What if someone like me were in charge of things, and yielded to this thought? I wonder if I'm doing a dangerous thing. I wonder...if almost anything can become a plague. I just thought you should keep it in mind. For the future.

LAWRENCE: I will.

GRAUNT: I stood there a long time, I think. Thinking. The sexton came back, without a doctor, and I asked him why, and he told me the doctor was dead.

LAWRENCE: What doctor?

GRAUNT: Edward Harman, did you know him?

(Pause)

LAWRENCE: Yes. I did, yes. He was my fr.... He was my physician. In fact. *(Pause)* Is there to be a funeral?

GRAUNT: Funerals are forbidden.

LAWRENCE: Do you know where the funeral is to be?

GRAUNT: Yes. I went there for the burial of the clerk.

LAWRENCE: Would you take me there?

GRAUNT: Yes.

LAWRENCE: Thank you. I would count it a favor.

GRAUNT: I would rather not hear the word "count."

(They cross up the steps and exit as the lights crossfade to:)

Scene Seven

(On the lower level: A few people enter, one by one, including LAWRENCE *and* GRAUNT. SARAH *enters quickly, looking from one face to another. She sees* LAWRENCE *and goes to him.)*

SARAH: Sir. You're the Lord Mayor, aren't you?

LAWRENCE: Yes.

SARAH: You hired me.

LAWRENCE: I remember. I sent you to work with Doctor Harman.

SARAH: Yes. I have a message for you.

LAWRENCE: From Doctor Harman? Did you nurse him as well?

SARAH: Before he went unconscious, he'd asked me to get him some wet cloths, and I was standing next to the bed, and.... And I'd thought I'd be able do it. He'd started to suffer, and I've seen so much of that, and he had asked me, but—

LAWRENCE: I don't understand, what had he asked you to do?

SARAH: He'd asked me to help him. Toward the end. I stood there next to the bed, but it was very hard for me to bring myself to do it, he must have seen how hard it was, all of a sudden one of his hands started grabbing at my wrist, his arm was tied down and he still made the reach, and I said, I'm trying to do it, Doctor Harman, he was panting for breath, the sores were in his throat, he couldn't get a word out, he took my wrist and drew a line across it with his finger, and another, and another, and I said, what do you want from me, and he drew a line between and then he drew a steeple and a funnel and a comb and what he was doing was spelling out I HAVE CHANGED MY MIND. (Pause) He lived for two days after that. It was very hard. But he was calmer toward the end, and he wrote on a slate. It took a long time. But what he said was to tell the Lord Mayor that he stayed. That he stayed the whole time.

(Pause)

LAWRENCE: You stayed there a long while, didn't you? Nursing him.

SARAH: A fair while, yes, Sir.

LAWRENCE: How do you feel?

SARAH: I'm a little tired. I think I'm going to rest here a while.

LAWRENCE: Thank you. Thank you for the message.

(VINCENT enters on the upper level, and stops at the sight of the crowd. They turn toward him.)

VINCENT: So. Here we are again. And so many. I came, every day I come, expecting to find no mourners left but myself. Sir John. Oh yes of course, he was a friend of yours. Shall we begin? I shall say a few words about Edward Harman and lead you in prayer. I should repeat that it is dangerous for you to be here. This place breathes infection. I confess I have wondered why we keep coming. But here we are, so let us begin, I should speak of Edward and recount his life.... Am I the only one who wonders why we come here? Why we keep on grieving?

Consider it. Nothing in the world eats the heart so much as grief. Love is such a powerful thing, that if it places any object in our hearts, we can scarcely bear it to be taken from us, without tearing our hearts in pieces. But still we can grieve. What gives us the strength? And think what we are asking when we grieve. What is the hope hidden in mourning? That our friend not be lost to us. That he breathe the living air, and join us again, for friendship's sake. That something, anything, rise from the dead. Yet we know this cannot happen. So why have we come?

If I could tell you some event of Edward's life and say, "This. This is how he became good...." But we never will know that. So what is left to say of him?

He worked here. He kept to his work. But I have already said this of hundreds....

Perhaps we should pray. Many have lost their faith by now, very many, the risen God was our hope, and hope is hard to recollect, like so many of our friends, so many burials, they blur together, all the dead.... But let us pray now, let us speak to God, shall we, of what is in our hearts. If we dare to speak such things.

Lord...what are we to do?

When the plague began, we thought we knew what you meant. We thought you were correcting us. So we tried to correct each other. We were wrong. What do you want of us now? Do you want us to acknowledge this world to be a hollow thing? Sir, we acknowledge it. We have learned what lies in our hollow places, we have smelt the corruption there. Are you punishing us? If so, then you know that we are punished now beyond our comprehension. Only a tyrant punishes the helpless beyond their comprehension. You know this.

We do not know what you want!

We gather in this graveyard every day. Today for Edward Harman, tomorrow for any of us. We no longer know why. But each day more die, we come out to the edge of the city and leave them here, we pray to you and go in again, and more die, and we come out here, and go in once more, and come out, and go in, and come out, and go in, it is unthinking, it is regular, it is constant. Like breathing.

Like the breath...

As if *we* were the breath of some great...living being....

Which has risen.

Brothers and sisters. Look at yourselves? Look what we have been made?

Go in peace.

(VINCENT *goes. Some of the crowd disperse.* GRAUNT *watches.* SARAH *is sitting on the steps. On the lower level,* BROUNKER *enters.*)

BROUNKER: Sir John! The most excellent news! Lady Castlemayne is delivered of a splendid boy. The King has acknowledged him, and named him Duke of Northumberland. The Court rejoices! In the midst of death, we are in life!

LAWRENCE: All of London salutes his majesty.

BROUNKER: I shall report it so.

LAWRENCE: And while you do, report this as well. If I do not receive the Poor Rate from any wealthy person, I shall instruct the constables to open his house and seize his property.

(Pause)

BROUNKER: You wouldn't.

LAWRENCE: Either I shall do it or the poor will do it.

BROUNKER: We will call out the army.

LAWRENCE: The army has the plague.

BROUNKER: You are a man of duty, Jack. You swore to do your utmost to preserve the city. Now you permit the city to be looted?

LAWRENCE: The city charter grants the Lord Mayor the power to collect the rates.

BROUNKER: I will report on this meeting to the court.

LAWRENCE: Do so. Please.

BROUNKER: Its information, but not its tone. The court well knows you are doing a hero's labor, a Herculean labor. Intemperance is permitted in our heroes.

LAWRENCE: Report whatever will make them act.

BROUNKER: Jack. Consider what you are doing. If you do this, if you strip the great houses to appease the poor, what becomes of your pledge to the King to preserve London?

(LAWRENCE looks at BROUNKER, and at GRAUNT.)

LAWRENCE: Sir, you may tell the King that my idea of what constitutes London has greatly changed.

(LAWRENCE turns and exits. BROUNKER watches him, then turns and exits the opposite way. GRAUNT starts to follow LAWRENCE, and stops.)

GRAUNT: Excuse me. Ma'am? Excuse me. We should go.

SARAH: Yes.

GRAUNT: It isn't safe to stay here, the smell is unhealthy.

SARAH: My family is here. *(Pause)* No one asks what happened to people, anymore.

GRAUNT: I do, actually. It's part of what I do.

SARAH: Why?

GRAUNT: I work with the Bills of Mortality.

SARAH: But they're wrong.

GRAUNT: Yes, I know.

SARAH: My husband didn't die of spotted fever.

(Pause)

GRAUNT: Shouldn't we go?

(Pause)

SARAH: I can't stand up.

GRAUNT: I'll get some help. Shall I get some help?

SARAH: We already buried the doctor. Now that he's dead— would you believe it? I think I'm the only person I know. Strange feeling. Like floating in the ether. (Pause) I don't feel well at all. (Pause) My name is Sarah Chandler, my husband's name was George Chandler, he died in Cripplegate parish, third of June. You could check the records, you could correct it. Anyone put down with spotted fever, smallpox. When they began punishing people for having the plague, we had to die of other things.

GRAUNT: I appreciate your telling me, Mrs Chandler.

SARAH: Well. You're trying to keep an inventory. I've kept inventory. (Pause) What's your name?

GRAUNT: Graunt. John Graunt, actually, if you— Fellow of the Royal Society.

SARAH: I'm pleased to meet you, Mr Graunt. You should leave now.

GRAUNT: Are you certain?

SARAH: I'll rest here for a while.

(GRAUNT looks at her for a moment. He turns, and looks up.)

GRAUNT: We knew so little. And we don't know much. So people ask me if we learned anything during the plague.

And I say we did. Newton did. He came up with something, just as I said, and he taught it to us. Those of us who lived. Plague spread to Cambridge, you see, and it closed for the duration, everyone scattered. Newton found himself on a lonely country estate. Nothing to do but take walks and think. One day, he walked in an apple orchard, noticed an apple fall to the earth.

Have you heard this story?

Looked at that apple. Really looked at it, no one had before, not really. Wondered what it meant. Wondered if he could describe what had happened mathematically. Tried. Did. Learned that when we fall to the earth, the earth also falls, a little, toward us. So that in fact there is no falling, but a moving toward. Tremendous thing. What Newton found: that the world would fly to pieces, but for a great force, a power in every single body in the world, which pulls it ceaselessly toward every other body, which is pulled ceaselessly toward it in turn. No matter what.

We learned what holds the world together, in the plague.

(GRAUNT *turns to look at* SARAH. *Then he crosses to her and holds out his hand. She looks at it. From the beginning of the play until this moment, no one has touched anyone else. She takes his hand and he helps her to stand and walk. The lights fade.*)

END OF PLAY

LET'S PLAY TWO

LET'S PLAY TWO was commissioned by South Coast Repertory. It was presented in South Coast Repertory's NewSCRipts series as a workshop directed by Barton DeLorenzo, and by the Playwrights' Center as a workshop directed by Kent Stephens.

The world premiere of LET'S PLAY TWO was presented on 22 September 1992 by South Coast Repertory, David Emmes, Producing Artistic Director, Martin Benson, Artistic Director. The cast and creative contributors were:

PHIL . . . . Arye Gross
GRACE . . . . .Susan Cash

Director . . . . Michael Bloom
Set . . . . .John Iacovelli
Lighting . . . . Brian Gale
Costumes . . . . .Dwight Richard Odle
Music and sound . . . . .Nathan Birnbaum
Stage manager . . . . Andy Tighe

ACKNOWLEDGMENTS

In addition to the above, my thanks also go to Jerry Patch, John Glore, Lisa Wasserman, and Robin Goodrin Nordli at South Coast Repertory, and to David Moore, Jeffrey Hatcher, J C Cutler, and Sally Wingert at the Playwrights' Center for their help in shaping the play.

I thank the John Simon Guggenheim Foundation, the McKnight Foundation, and the Playwrights' Center for their generous financial support during the writing of LET'S PLAY TWO.

CHARACTERS

GRACE, age 34
PHIL, age 27

TIME AND PLACE

Minnesota and elsewhere. Baseball season, 1991.

SET

Something suggesting a car. A piece of open road that rapidly becomes several different rooms defined by a single piece of furniture. Enough space to dance in.

I see great things in baseball. It's our game—the American game. It will take our people out-of-doors, fill them with oxygen, give them a larger physical stoicism. Tend to relieve us from being a nervous, dyspeptic set. Repair these losses, and be a blessing to us.

Walt Whitman

It's a great day for a ballgame. Let's play two!

Ernie Banks

ACT ONE

Scene One

(A horn honks. Lights up on PHIL *sitting in the car, wearing a serviceable dark blue suit. The engine is running. His door is open, he's leaning out and looking up.)*

PHIL: Grace? *(He honks the horn again.)* Grace! We're running late!

GRACE: *(Off)* Coming!

PHIL: You want me to come up?

GRACE: Down in a sec!

*(*PHIL *shuts the door and turns on the radio. He flips through the static along the dial until he finds a song he likes. The rhythm is a deep pounding and a higher, faster sound. The vocals are sampled and scratched and hard to make out. He turns up the volume and taps the steering wheel.)*

*(*GRACE *runs in, wearing an overcoat over a large dress we can't see. She opens the passenger door, slides in, and slams the door.)*

GRACE: Drive like hell.

(They kiss. While they do, PHIL *feels for the radio and turns it to an oldies station.)*

GRACE: Thank you.

(The kiss goes on.)

PHIL: Aren't you hot in that?

GRACE: Don't start.

PHIL: Why not?

GRACE: We're gonna be late. You know what happens.

PHIL: I like what happens.

*(*GRACE *pulls away.)*

GRACE: Drive. The car.

PHIL: I'll drive the car.

*(*PHIL *pulls into traffic. They get themselves straightened out.)*

GRACE: Good morning.

PHIL: Good morning. Did they give you a map?

GRACE: I've got directions.

PHIL: They didn't put in one of those little slips of paper with the cartoon map on it? What kind of wedding invitation is that?

GRACE: Julia—that's the bride—

PHIL: Julia—bride. The bride's name is Julia. Okay. I've gotta get all this before we get there.

GRACE: You'll have plenty of time. Why does being a bride give you permission to go insane? It hadn't really sunk in— Look at these directions. They're two pages long. Do you have a map?

PHIL: Sure, somewhere.

GRACE: Of the entire Midwest? She said she wanted the ceremony by a lake, I thought no problem, it's Minnesota—

PHIL: Ten thousand lakes, plenty to go around.

GRACE: I think she picked Lake Tanganyika.

PHIL: Source of the Nile? Excellent choice. I'll need to stop for gas.

GRACE: Sorry about this.

PHIL: Believe me, I love a long drive.

GRACE: Do you think anyone saw what I'm wearing under this?

PHIL: I can't even see it.

GRACE: Good.

PHIL: What does it look like?

GRACE: It's a bridesmaid's dress. It looks like a Halloween costume. Wave to the Metrodome.

PHIL: Hello, Dome!

GRACE: World's biggest diaphragm.

PHIL: Goodbye, Dome!

GRACE: Wish you were here!

PHIL: That's what we should do, blow this off and go to a game.

GRACE: They're playing in Kansas City.

PHIL: I know. Talkin' 'bout a road trip. (Singing) Oh, I'm going to Kansas City, Kansas City here I come—everybody!— They've got some overpaid relief pitchers there—

GRACE: *(Singing)* And I'm gonna get me one.

PHIL: All right! A bow bow bow bow...

GRACE: I appreciate you going to this with me. You're very brave.

PHIL: It's nothing.

GRACE: You're the first man I've known who'd be my date at a wedding.

PHIL: Why?

GRACE: God, you're young.

PHIL: Shut up. What's wrong with weddings? It's a one-, maybe two-stop date. All the usual dating questions, poof! Gone! "Geez, what'll I wear?" Blue suit, no problem. "Entertainment?" The ceremony! I laughed, I cried. "Where do we eat?" End of the hall, sir, Ballroom Number Two. "Do we go for drinks?" Champagne punch, there you go. "Dancing?" Sleazy little cover band, at your service. And the killer: "Will she wind up in a romantic mood?" Well, I think we both know the answer to that one.

GRACE: And I even paid for the gift.

PHIL: I'm telling you, it's great. Come on, you love weddings.

GRACE: Love weddings? No.

PHIL: Then why do you go to so many?

GRACE: I get invited. Somebody you care for goes through something big, it's your duty to be there for them.

PHIL: You make it sound like chemotherapy. That can't be why.

GRACE: Look, it's different from your idea of a good time.

PHIL: Tell me.

GRACE: I stare at the bride. She's standing there, and you forget that she made you buy a two hundred-dollar red taffeta ball gown for a daytime lakeshore wedding. She's wearing that long white dress, it's as bright as a movie screen, you stare at it, and your eyes.... It's weird.

PHIL: What?

GRACE: I start watching movies on her. All the times I've known her. We're all standing there, her family and the groom and the priest, and I'm watching the bride crawl all over some frat boy you can bet she never mentioned to any of them. Then I see her in the snow pushing a hatchback full of everything I own. Now she's practically shoving me at her brother, who back in real life is ten feet away in a bad tuxedo. Now she's laughing till snot comes out of her nose. Now she's introducing a guy. She's got this bright animal look that says, "Please just tell me he's perfect." And now she's standing next to the guy. Wearing a wedding gown. And soon I'm gonna watch her go away. So you cry a little. And that's what I do at weddings. You asked.

PHIL: You're a way more serious person than I am.

GRACE: I'm sorry.

PHIL: No! I learn a lot. I've never done that.

GRACE: What do you do at a wedding?

PHIL: Point at the groom and laugh. Were you doing that at Bob and Cindy's wedding?

GRACE: Yes, and I was doing that at Kyle and Suzannah's wedding.

PHIL: Here we go—

GRACE: Where we met.

PHIL: We met at Bob and Cindy's wedding.

GRACE: We met at Kyle and Suzannah's—I asked you and some other guy to move a couch out of the dressing room. I can't believe you don't remember something from eight weeks ago.

PHIL: I'm supposed to remember that? Some lady in a big dress asks me to move a couch?

GRACE: Yes, you are supposed to remember that. "Some lady?"

(GRACE *takes a compact from her purse and looks at herself.*)

PHIL: You okay?

GRACE: Do I look like I'm not okay?

PHIL: You look great.

GRACE: I look green. God, who does your makeup, Earl Scheib?

PHIL: Hey. I got to *know* you at Bob and Cindy's wedding. Six weeks ago. And then of course we mmhmhmhmhm after Kurt and Shelley's wedding. Five weeks ago. See, I remember this stuff. Hey, let me ask you—this thing where you look at the bride. Do you do this a lot?

GRACE: Only with people I care for.

PHIL: Huh. You just look at her—

(GRACE *leaves the car and enters a different light, with talk and laughter and music in the background.*)

PHIL: And you see her doing things from before?

(PHIL *crosses toward* GRACE, *who is sitting and staring. She wears a far-too-elaborate bridesmaid's gown. The sounds of a baseball broadcast, audible but indistinct.*)

GRACE: Come on, come on...

PHIL: Hello?

GRACE: Sorry?

PHIL: Are the, uh—

GRACE: Hi.

PHIL: Do you know where they've put the coats?

GRACE: No.

PHIL: Oh. Sorry, hi. I'm Phil. Some wedding, huh?

GRACE: Some kind of wedding. Grace, yeah, nice to see you again.

PHIL: Doesn't Cindy look great?

GRACE: Especially compared to what she made the bridesmaids wear.

PHIL: Really, no, you look—

GRACE: *(Reacting to something she sees)* Oh, Jesus!

PHIL: You okay?

GRACE: Fine. Thanks.

PHIL: You sure?

GRACE: Yeah. Little spasm, there.

PHIL: Are you having, uh—should I tell anyone...?

GRACE: No, no—

PHIL: Get you anything?

GRACE: No.

PHIL: Is the T V bothering you?

GRACE: No! Uh, that's okay...

PHIL: Hey! That's the Twins game!

GRACE: Oh, yeah, so it is. I'm okay, I'll come back in a minute.

PHIL: He's bunting! Come on, he's gonna—beats it out, damn—

GRACE: Shit, Aguilera, field your position! *(Pause)* It happened to be on, so I've been, uh... *(Pause)* Cindy thinks I have cramps, don't tell, okay?

PHIL: Sure. What's the score?

GRACE: Three to two Minnesota, bottom of the ninth, one away. Did she throw the bouquet yet?

PHIL: Yeah.

GRACE: Who caught it?

PHIL: Cathy.

GRACE: Cathy who?

PHIL: Cathy my date.

GRACE: Uh-huh. And you're in here because...?

PHIL: I was looking for the coats.

GRACE: Sure.

PHIL: No, really—

GRACE: Come on, Rick.

PHIL: Okay, Ricky, blow it by him. Why are *you* in here?

GRACE: We're in a pennant race. This is an important game.

PHIL: The season opened a week ago.

GRACE: Christ almighty, hangs the curve—

PHIL: Goes...foul. I mean, it's April.

GRACE: You should see me in September. When people start to say, "What happened to this season?" I'll be thinking, "Remember that close one back in April?" It comes back to *me*.

PHIL: Ohhh. When you said this was an important game, you didn't mean compared to other games, you meant compared to everything else.

GRACE: I meant it was a game of *baseball*. They're probably about to leave, huh?

PHIL: After this inning we'll throw rice at Cindy.

GRACE: They're using rose petals.

PHIL: I bet if you ball those up real tight, you could throw them pretty hard.

GRACE: Now you're talking. Come on, Rick, ground ball to the left.

PHIL: Throw the double-play ball.

GRACE: Yes!

PHIL: Six! To four!

GRACE: Pivots! Throws!

PHIL: To three!

GRACE: Digs it out!

PHIL: Double play!

GRACE: God above, that's a beautiful thing.

(The lights crossfade as they cross toward the car.)

PHIL: You want to maybe—

GRACE: Yeah, we'd better.

PHIL: I'm Phil, in case you—

GRACE: Grace. Hi.

(The lights change to:)

Scene Two

(Car interior, daylight. Engine sounds and wind. PHIL is driving. GRACE is crouched, contorted, in the back seat, attempting to remove a very large dress without being seen by passing cars. This is difficult.)

PHIL: Huh.

GRACE: Did you say something?

PHIL: No.

GRACE: I'm gonna kill Julia.

PHIL: We'll get there.

GRACE: In a scarlet taffeta ballgown with great big sweat stains.

PHIL: So take it off, put it back on when we get there.

GRACE: What the hell do you think I'm doing back here, Greco-Roman wrestling? Have you ever tried getting out of three crinoline skirts in a compact car?

PHIL: No.

GRACE: You haven't lived.

PHIL: So I've been thinking about what you said.

GRACE: Which?

PHIL: When you look at someone you care about.

GRACE: What, like at weddings?

PHIL: Yeah. How come that's never happened to me before?

GRACE: Couldn't tell you.

PHIL: Huh. So I told you I ran into Cathy?

(*All motion ceases in the back seat.* GRACE *pokes her head up.*)

GRACE: No, you didn't.

PHIL: Didn't I? Sure, I did.

GRACE: Nooo, I would have remembered.

PHIL: Oh. Well, I did. She dropped off the last of my stuff.

GRACE: Nice of her.

PHIL: Yeah, I was surprised.

GRACE: Then what happened?

PHIL: Oh, you know. I've been trying to figure out why she and I didn't work out. I mean, I'm glad we didn't, obviously, 'cause....

GRACE: Because...?

PHIL: But I think I took it harder than I thought.

(GRACE *cautiously goes back to changing.*)

GRACE: You were together how long?

PHIL: Hang on...ten days.

GRACE: Ten—

PHIL: Wait, is that right?

GRACE: How did I get the idea that Cathy was a major relationship?

PHIL: She was.

GRACE: I've had colds that lasted longer.

PHIL: We lived together.

GRACE: How long, a week?

PHIL: About. Look, it's a long story.

GRACE: Can't be that long.

PHIL: I moved in on our anniversary, and then, I don't know, the romance went out of it.

GRACE: So. Cathy came over...

PHIL: Gave me back my stuff, we talked over old times—

GRACE: Old times?

PHIL: Are you okay?

GRACE: I have a pounding headache.

PHIL: Have you taken something for it?

GRACE: No.

PHIL: Well, could you?

GRACE: In a minute. Are you sorry you and Cathy broke up?

PHIL: No! But I think it was two things. One was the day I got home and she asked me to pick the mattress off the kitchen floor and move it back to the bedroom. I understood, her Mom was coming over, but...I didn't care who knew.

GRACE: Why'd you move the bed into the kitchen?

PHIL: So there'd be one less reason to ever get up. Eating, working, sports, all that, bathroom breaks, I thought it ought to feel like we were still in bed. After that it was never the same.

GRACE: How old are you again?

PHIL: Twenty-seven.

GRACE: Okay, yeah. So that was the first thing, what was the second thing?

PHIL: We were driving home from Bob and Cindy's wedding and Cathy asked me did I notice that she had caught the bouquet and where did I disappear to for so long and why did I give a high-five to the woman who knocked Cindy's hat off with a wad of rose petals.

(GRACE *grins and disappears behind the seat.*)

PHIL: It turned out that she doesn't like baseball.

(PHIL *adjusts the rearview mirror downward.*)

GRACE: Hey. What are you doing?

PHIL: Looking at you.

GRACE: Eyes on the road, driver.

PHIL: You know? Maybe there was a third thing. I thought I was in love with her. But...when I looked at her...

GRACE: Which I gather was mostly from *very* close up—

PHIL: I just looked at her. I didn't picture her from any other times.

GRACE: Not a lot of other times to choose from.

PHIL: Huh. So you think I've never done that 'cause I haven't loved anyone *long* enough. (*He's looking at her.*) But that can't be why, because...

(GRACE *leaves the car and enters a different light. She has on a nice blouse and skirt and wears an I D tag with a store logo.*)

GRACE: Look out!

(A baseball comes flying through the fourth wall. GRACE ducks out of the way. The roar of the crowd, the crack of the bat. Bright lights, strongly frontal. GRACE is in a skybox in the Hubert Humphrey Metrodome. PHIL scrambles after the ball and joins her.)

PHIL: Holy shit!

GRACE: How did he do that!

(PHIL retrieves the ball and holds it up.)

PHIL: Right here! Gladden! Right here!

GRACE: (Adrenalined) That was a foul tip! He didn't even get good wood on the ball and it flies all the way into a skybox! I've seen a million foul balls, but you're in this living room, it's like he hit it out of the T V.

PHIL: Having a good time so far?

GRACE: Beats the hell out of what I usually do after work. Does this always happen, you walk through the door and they hit a ball in your lap?

PHIL: Ah, you get used to it. I'm kidding, you think I rate this all the time? Marketing reserved it, cancelled at the last minute, Jack my boss had dibs, he's out of town, so I grabbed it. Do you want some food?

(GRACE unclips her I D tag and slips it in a pocket as she looks down at the crowd.)

GRACE: Not right now. (She does a double-take.) Hey, that—

PHIL: What?

GRACE: Nothing, no way, sorry.

PHIL: You okay?

GRACE: My brain must be fried. All the old people in baseball caps—sheesh, that weirds me out—I thought I saw my Mom.

PHIL: Does she go to a lot of games?

GRACE: She died years ago.

PHIL: Oh. Huh.

GRACE: What?

PHIL: No, just—"If you build it, she will—"

GRACE: Oh, shut up. So is it gonna be just us?

PHIL: I left a bunch of messages. Pretty short notice, though.

GRACE: Will—sorry, I don't remember her name—will she be here? Your date at the wedding.

PHIL: Cathy. No. We broke up, actually.

GRACE: Oh. I'm—The wedding was five days ago, when did this happen?

PHIL: Five days ago.

GRACE: Oh. Yikes.

(PHIL *holds up a Twins baseball cap.*)

PHIL: Hey. Do you think this'll fit a four-year-old girl? I haven't seen her in a while, but it seems really big.

GRACE: Should be okay. Who's it for?

PHIL: My niece. (*He pulls out other souvenirs.*) The pennants are for the nephews. Check out the Twins romper suit.

GRACE: How many nieces and nephews do you have?

(PHIL *reaches for his wallet and flips through pictures.*)

PHIL: These are my brother's kids—Joshua, he's five, he's in accelerated kindergarten, and Jason, he's three, he's supposed to look like me but I don't see it. Here's my sister's kids—Jody's the four-year-old, she just hit the horsey stage, and Jeremiah's about to be one.

(GRACE *isn't looking at the pictures, she's looking at* PHIL.)

GRACE: You like children.

PHIL: Well...sure, you know.

(PHIL *glances fondly at the pictures and puts the wallet away.*)

GRACE: Oh, come on.

PHIL: What?

GRACE: Cut it out, seriously.

PHIL: What?

GRACE: Nothing. Never mind.

(*Pause*)

PHIL: I can't believe nobody else has shown up.

GRACE: It does seem strange, yeah.

(*Pause*)

PHIL: Oh! Okay. Jeez, I'm an idiot! You think I set this up. I told you there'd be a crowd and so far it's only me. You're thinking what if it's a date and you didn't know! I feel like an idiot!

GRACE: You feel—I walk in the door and in two minutes' time you tell me you're unattached and you love kids. How am I supposed to feel? I mean,

Jesus, I'm only thirty-four, I'm not standing outside the sperm bank with a little tin cup just yet.

(Pause)

PHIL: You're thirty-four?

GRACE: Say well-preserved or anything like it, you're a dead man.

PHIL: Did some guy do something to you that I should know about so I don't even start to do it?

GRACE: No one in particular. Do you think it would take the exceptional cruelty of one particular man to make me a little cautious?

(Uh-oh. They turn quickly back to the game.)

PHIL: Aaand Gladden gets the base on balls.

(Long awkward pause. Then GRACE *does a double-take.)*

GRACE: Lord! Do you ever have one of those days where everyone you see, you mistake them for somebody you know? There's no way my Dad's here.

PHIL: Is he dead, too?

GRACE: No, but he only went to games on all his visitation days with me.

PHIL: You luckout.

GRACE: I asked him once did he think there was any chance Harmon Killebrew was my real father.

PHIL: Ow. What did he do?

GRACE: He said he wouldn't be a bit surprised. God, was I a stinker.

PHIL: Hey. Help me out here. You would know this.

GRACE: What?

PHIL: Who is that?

GRACE: Chuck Knoblauch. Rookie, second base.

PHIL: I know. But what you were saying. Who *is* that?

GRACE: Who does he remind you—?

PHIL: Whose batting stance is that?

GRACE: You're right—

PHIL: Charlie Lau style—

GRACE: Yeah, the head, but look at the wrists.

PHIL: Vertical bat, head down, who is that?

GRACE: Why am I thinking Red Sox?

PHIL: Yes!

GRACE: Boggs? No.

PHIL: Greenwell.

GRACE: You think?

PHIL: No.

GRACE: Jody—?

PHIL: Jody Reed.

GRACE: It's Jody Reed.

PHIL: Plain as day.

GRACE: Huh. Everybody's here.

(PHIL *puts up his hand.* GRACE *slaps it in a high-five. Their hands stay attached. They're still looking at each other. The crowd roars.*)

PHIL: Watch it!

(PHIL *and* GRACE *duck out of the way as a baseball comes flying through the fourth wall.* PHIL *goes scrambling after it.*)

GRACE: Jesus!

PHIL: Yes! Amazing!

GRACE: Jesus Christ!

(PHIL *retrieves the ball and holds it up to wave to the crowd.*)

PHIL: Chuck! You god! I want your autograph!

(*The crowd roars.*)

GRACE: What are the odds that it—what are the—

PHIL: This is why you come to the park!

GRACE: Jesus H—

PHIL: The game is live!

GRACE: Right by our—

PHIL: We are live!

(*The lights fade fast.*)

Scene Three

(Car interior, daylight. Engine sounds and wind.)

PHIL: Are you okay?

GRACE: Been better.

PHIL: I didn't know you got carsick.

GRACE: Me neither. There, Highway 210, that's our next turn, one mile. Great, only one and a half pages of Julia's goddamn directions to go.

PHIL: So I want to ask you about something.

GRACE: Okay.

PHIL: And I need you to try not to get angry.

GRACE: I'll try.

PHIL: Because it's kind of complicated.

GRACE: I'll try, all *right*? Highway 210, three quarters of a mile.

PHIL: Got it.

GRACE: So talk to me.

PHIL: Okay. I really like you.

GRACE: Well. I really like you, too.

PHIL: Okay. That's great. Okay.

GRACE: Is this about Cathy?

PHIL: Kind of.

GRACE: I knew it.

PHIL: And other people, too.

GRACE: Other women.

PHIL: Yeah. No, God, not "other women" like The Other Woman, just—women. From the past.

GRACE: Dolley Madison? Mamie Eisenhower?

PHIL: I'm trying to tell you something that's painful and revealing for me to say, and we thank you for your support!

GRACE: I'm sorry. Half a mile to Highway 210. You were saying.

PHIL: Maybe another time.

GRACE: Tell me now. Please.

PHIL: You've got to let me concentrate a little. Don't get angry right away?

GRACE: Go ahead.

PHIL: See, when it comes to women—

GRACE: Already I'm angry.

PHIL: I just started.

GRACE: Swell.

PHIL: I'm trying to be honest with you.

GRACE: Well, thank God for *that*, I mean thank God that the horrible statement I see on the horizon here isn't a *fabrication*.

PHIL: So when it comes to women, I—

GRACE: Phil? When speaking to a woman, try not to say, "When it comes to women." Quarter of a mile, coming right up.

PHIL: When it comes to...my relationships. I think I've gotten way too... goal-oriented. There's a checklist by now. First glance and look away. First talk. First laugh. First little flirtation. First phone call, first lunch, first heavy conversation. First date, first touch, first kiss, first dance, first awful true confession. First day together, sleep together, night together, morning together, meeting each others' friends together, first big fight. First screaming multiple orgasm—

GRACE: *Thank* you okay. Thank you for sharing. These women. Once you've done these things. What happens?

PHIL: That's the thing. After that I run out of ideas.

GRACE: You run out of ideas. That's the list.

PHIL: Pretty much.

GRACE: And after that, after *that* list—

PHIL: I'm sure I left out a few things.

GRACE: Hoo boy. And now?

PHIL: Now?

GRACE: Yeah.

PHIL: I guess I'm wondering what's the point.

GRACE: Shit. Did we exit?

PHIL: What?

GRACE: Did you take the exit?

PHIL: I think so.

GRACE: I don't think you did. You drove right by it.

PHIL: I was trying to put something important into words.

GRACE: Fine, that's great, now put the car into reverse.

PHIL: Did it make sense, what I was—

GRACE: It made perfect sense, now turn the car around!

PHIL: I'll turn around when I get another exit! I'll be taking Highway 210, right?

GRACE: 210 East.

PHIL: Great. West, though, right? 'Cause we're coming from the other way.

GRACE: We still have to go east.

PHIL: That's right. But it's a left now.

GRACE: Right.

PHIL: Okay. So. After Cathy and I broke up, I thought, great, fine, I'll just find somebody else.

GRACE: Can we stop for a moment to consider all the assumptions behind "I'll just find somebody else?"

PHIL: Sure. I go out, I drink, play games, watch sports, go to work, find somebody else. There are a lot of Cathies out there. Then what? It used to be an adventure to meet someone new. Lately it's a commute.

GRACE: And now...

PHIL: I really like you.

GRACE: Right, got that, good.

PHIL: And I don't know what to do.

GRACE: Do.

PHIL: Yeah.

GRACE: Oh God. Okay. Yeah. It's been great. We'll talk sometime.

PHIL: No, see—

GRACE: No, you're right, we won't talk sometime. We won't do a thing, this is it, you've run out of ideas. You were a person I wanted to be with and meanwhile I'm a bunch of things you wanted to do.

PHIL: I knew you'd get angry.

GRACE: Get out. Get out of here.

PHIL: We're going seventy miles an hour.

GRACE: Better yet.

PHIL: What did I do?

GRACE: One: You're getting us lost. Two: You're trying to break something to me, and I wish you'd get it over with.

PHIL: One: I am turning around. Two: I'm not trying to break anything to you, I'm saying I don't know what to do about how I feel.

GRACE: Fine, I heard that.

PHIL: So I'm asking for suggestions.

GRACE: You call that a list? Me and some guys have gotten through that list in a weekend.

PHIL: Huh.

GRACE: You want some real goals, Phil? When does he start talking to me every day? When does he stop wanting to see anybody else? When does he meet my godawful family? When does he start making some plans? When does he want to change his life? What if something happens?

(Pause)

PHIL: So you think I have the wrong list.

GRACE: It's a wee bit limited.

PHIL: Huh. I was thinking what's wrong was having a list.

(GRACE turns to look at him. She smiles. The lights start to change. Music comes in, low: a small band playing a big band dance tune.)

PHIL: 'Cause I think what I'm trying to say is—

GRACE: Uh-oh.

(GRACE snaps her head to the front. The lights and sound snap back to normal.)

PHIL: You okay?

GRACE: Yeah. My eyes were just...weird. *(She's trying to not look quite at him.)* Look, before I hear any more I'm gonna need to find a drugstore. Okay?

PHIL: Sure. 'Cause I think we missed the exit again.

GRACE: Oh, for God's sake.

PHIL: I'm sorry.

GRACE: No, I'm sorry. I should have planned better, I shouldn't have picked today to feel so cruddy, you're being—very nice.

PHIL: I'm having a good time.

GRACE: I'm not always like this, you know? We've had fun sometimes.

PHIL: We have.

GRACE: I'll be more fun again soon.

PHIL: Relax. You're giving me a chance to feel relatively mature.

GRACE: *(Giving him a look)* You? You wish.

(The lights and music come up again. PHIL *crosses downstage onto a dance floor, doing a formless sort of freestyle boogaloo.)*

PHIL: I love dancing! You'd never know it to look at me.

*(*GRACE *crosses to him. She is wearing another godawful bridesmaid's gown.)*

PHIL: I still think that's a nice dress.

GRACE: I'm gonna kill Shelley.

PHIL: Hey, it's 'way better than the thing Cindy made you wear.

GRACE: You told me you liked that.

PHIL: Well, I like this better. It looks nice on you.

GRACE: Friendship is based on trust.

PHIL: I meant that I like your shoulders.

GRACE: Oh. By the way, this is a tango. What are you doing?

PHIL: That's amazing. You know an actual dance?

GRACE: It's just a tango. Like this. *(She dances for a couple of bars, well.)* Nobody ever sent you to dance class?

PHIL: I don't know anyone who can do a dance with a name.

GRACE: Oh, come on.

PHIL: Look around the room. Huh? Disaster area.

GRACE: I got sent to these classes where we learned steps to music that no one with a brain would play anymore. Jesus, I feel like the chaperone.

PHIL: Teach it to me.

GRACE: This is embarrassing.

PHIL: You could try. Come on.

GRACE: Okay, come here. And...

(They try, and fail.)

PHIL: Tell you what. You do the tango and I'll do what I do.

(They do: she tangos across the floor as he dances freestyle around her, shaping the space around her and making "tah-dah" gestures behind her moves. She has trouble keeping a straight face.)

GRACE: You're not supposed to smile when you do the tango.

(His dance assumes a few tangolike poses. She makes a few "tah-dah" moves.)

PHIL: Yes! The Kid is dancing!

(The music ends. Clapping.)

GRACE: The Kid?

PHIL: Me, sort of. Thing I do. It's kind of dumb.

GRACE: Tell me.

PHIL: Like, if I've got dishes to do, I'll say, "The Kid is stepping up to the sink, Red! He's using Lemon Joy and a wood-handled brush in there, Vin. Would you look at the scrubbing technique on the Kid!"

GRACE: Why "the Kid?"

PHIL: It's what my Dad used to call me. I turned it into something fun.

GRACE: I've heard of making up imaginary playmates. You made up E S P N.

PHIL: My brother and sister are way older than me. I think I was an accident. Something my Dad said.... I asked my Mom, and she said, "Maybe an accident, but certainly not a mistake."

GRACE: Yay, Mom.

PHIL: Yeah, good save. Anyway, I played alone a lot.

(A mirror ball descends and is hit by colored lights. The band starts a slow one.)

GRACE: Oh, my God...

PHIL: Awright! Slow dance!

GRACE: I'm with a sixteen-year-old.

(They start doing a waltz-type thing, which gradually decays into the swaying vertical hug of high-school dances. He grins at her. She looks at him.)

GRACE: What?

PHIL: What?

GRACE: What am I doing funny?

PHIL: Nothing. What am I doing?

GRACE: You're grinning again.

PHIL: *(Trying to straighten his face)* Still?

GRACE: Not so much.

PHIL: Now? Better?

(They are looking at each other with very serious expressions. GRACE begins to crack first, which starts PHIL, and GRACE makes a little sputtery sound, and it's all over, they're grinning and laughing. Then they just look at each other.)

PHIL: Wow.

GRACE: Hm. You know, we could—

PHIL: I bet we could.

GRACE: Yeah?

PHIL: Oh, yeah.

(They look around and stealthily sidle away, back toward the car. As they go, the lights crossfade to:)

Scene Four

(Daylight. PHIL and GRACE in the car.)

GRACE: No!

PHIL: What!

GRACE: Look at the road signs.

PHIL: What?

GRACE: Half the words are French.

PHIL: Huh.

GRACE: Tell me we're not in Canada, Phil.

PHIL: No way.

GRACE: Canada or New Orleans, take your pick. Phil, we are seriously lost. We're not gonna make it. God, what is Julia gonna think?

PHIL: Do you have a number where the wedding's going to be?

GRACE: I called from the drugstore, I got a machine.

PHIL: This is ridiculous. They expect you to find this place in the middle of the wilderness, you're sick as a dog, it's probably over already.

GRACE: Plus we've been driving in every direction but the right one for hours.

PHIL: What do you want to do? You want me to drive you home?

GRACE: I hate to break it to you, Phil, but what I want is for you to ask someone for directions.

PHIL: Aw, hell.

GRACE: *(Moaning)* Oh. Oh God.

PHIL: Still feeling bad?

GRACE: Uh-huh.

PHIL: What did you get at the drugstore, didn't it help?

GRACE: Uh-uh.

PHIL: *(Pointing)* Here! What you need is some solid food. Soft drink, fix you right up. Huh? We'll go to the drive-thru window. Do you know what you want?

GRACE: I want to die.

PHIL: I'll order first.

(A preposterous plastic cartoon thing with a speaker inside appears next to the car. PHIL leans out the window.)

PHIL: Hi!

(Unintelligible static)

PHIL: Uh, howdy. Could I get a western bacon double cheeseburger, and, let's see, the ranch-style fries—

(GRACE is quietly overcome by a feral alertness, going very still except for her eyes.)

PHIL: —that's a large, and some extra barbeque sauce with that would be great. Grace? You know what you want? Mushroom burger?

GRACE: Start without me. *(She grabs her purse and exits fast.)*

PHIL: Grace? I think my friend is heading inside, I'll come in for it, all right? Listen, is there anything on the menu you'd recommend for somebody with an upset stomach? McSoda Crackers or something?

(A toilet flushes. The lights crossfade to:)

(GRACE is standing in the restroom. Hard, fluorescent lights, sound of running water and through the wall the clash of kitchen trays. In one hand she is holding, gingerly, the small plastic cup and testing stick from a pregnancy test kit. The cup is full. In the other hand she holds the instructions, which she is reading with fierce concentration.)

GRACE: Please. Please. Shit, Grace, who are you talking to? *(She looks around and shrinks a little. She takes a deep breath, pulls the testing stick from the cup, and watches it.)* Just—please. Be pink. Okay? Please. Not pregnant. Hey, little guy. Don't be blue? Huh? Be pink. And then later, you know? Later you can be anything you want. Just be pink for me now. Huh? Huh? Come on, you can tell I'm not ready for this, I'm talking to plastic. Which is Dodger blue. God damn it! I don't even know what country I'm in. How did this happen?

(*Seductive music.* GRACE *watches as* PHIL *enters, dragging a mattress with a bottomsheet, a couple of pillows, and a comforter.*)

GRACE: Okay, right. It comes back to me.

(*Lights down on* GRACE *as* PHIL *pulls off his shirt and necktie.* PHIL *hops on one foot, as he kicks his shoes off. The bridesmaid's dress comes flying in.* PHIL *undoes his pants.*)

(GRACE *strolls on, wrapped in a sheet, and meets* PHIL *at the foot of the mattress.* PHIL *takes one corner of the sheet, and* GRACE *does a pirouette, unwinding it. They are both upstage of the sheet.*)

GRACE: (*To the music*) Two, three—

(*They fall onto the mattress together, landing in positions of postcoital languor. After a moment,* PHIL *leans up wearily on an elbow and gropes for a roll of toilet paper. He tears some off, reaches under the covers, makes a face, gives a pull and a couple of swabs. The hand reemerges with the paper in a crumpled ball.*)

PHIL: The Kid steps to the free throw line, he sets his stance... (*He tosses the ball of tissue offstage.*) Swish! The Kid completes the three-point play and we're going to overtime!

(GRACE *rolls toward him and makes a face.*)

GRACE: Man, that stuff gets cold in a hurry.

PHIL: Don't look at me, mine are in the trash trying to impregnate a condom—

(*She peeks under the top sheet.*)

GRACE: No way this is all me.

PHIL: —I picture them beating their tiny heads against the walls, going, (*He pulls the top sheet tightly over his head.*) "Grace! Grace! Grace!"

GRACE: I was really having a time.

PHIL: Hi.

GRACE: Mmmm.

PHIL: How are you?

GRACE: Hee hee hee.

PHIL: Really?

GRACE: Hee hee hee hee hee.

PHIL: That's, uh...

GRACE: Yeah?

PHIL: This has been a very pleasant evening and I'm not just saying that.

(They chortle.)

PHIL: Did you doze off?

GRACE: God, I must have.

PHIL: Can I imagine that you passed out cold?

GRACE: Whatever.

(He holds up a hand.)

PHIL: Big high-five for the Kid?

GRACE: There are times I envy you so much it could kill me.

PHIL: I've done something wrong here. I can tell.

GRACE: You're not wrong, but.... Yes you are. You're wrong. I come more than once, it's a tribute to *you*. Mister Prowess *made* me come. *You* come more than once, it's also a tribute to you.

PHIL: I have this concern about.... I just want you to be pleased.

GRACE: I was pleased. Really pleased.

(Pause)

PHIL: I've been thinking. How would you feel about moving in together?

GRACE: Phil. That is an incredibly sweet suggestion.

PHIL: That isn't a "yes," I guess, huh?

GRACE: You want to get through a woman as quick as you can, don'tcha?

PHIL: What do you mean?

GRACE: Sweetie, you've been *thinking* about this? Since when? Five seconds ago? Ten? It's just.... Most people, they talk about moving in together, it's a commitment. With you, it's a second date. What's the rush?

PHIL: I guess.

GRACE: Have I hurt your feelings?

PHIL: No. I'm okay.

GRACE: Listen, I'd better get going. If I stay here longer, Mister Prowess will render me useless for the workday.

PHIL: Yeah?

GRACE: Get some sleep. And thank you for a lovely time. You pile-driving marathon sex god.

PHIL: Look at the sexual technique on the Kid!

(GRACE *laughs, and starts gathering up her clothes.*)

PHIL: What's he using in there, Red? Well, those are male genitalia, Vin. The Kid is earning some big bucks from product endorsements for those genitals, isn't he, Red? Yes, Vin, and it's a disturbing trend, teenagers are shooting each other over those penises.... You don't have to go.

GRACE: I have to get to work in a few hours.

PHIL: So do I, so? Blow it off.

GRACE: Come on.

PHIL: I mean it.

GRACE: Walk me to my car?

(*She starts to get dressed. He's staring into space. She stops, and looks at him.*)

GRACE: Phil? How are things at work?

PHIL: Oh, Lordy.

GRACE: Phil? How's work, Phil?

PHIL: Work. Work has been kind of...not.

(*He starts getting dressed.*)

GRACE: Phil. You didn't.

PHIL: You know what they wanted me to do? Last week I met with the people on one of our assembly floors to tell them about their wonderful new flexible benefit plan. This week my boss wanted me to go back and tell them about their severance pay. Every one of those guys would have thought I knew all along they were screwed.

GRACE: Did you know?

PHIL: No! My boss has stopped telling me stuff in advance. He knows I'm a bad liar, so he doesn't trust me anymore.

GRACE: So you quit.

PHIL: No—

GRACE: You made a big fiery speech to your boss and you quit.

PHIL: I made a big fiery speech to the mirror and called in sick.

GRACE: What are you going to do?

PHIL: I'll get another job.

GRACE: You'll just get another—nobody's getting other jobs!

PHIL: I always have.

GRACE: Always? Have you done this kind of thing a lot?

PHIL: My jobs always go bad. It's awful.

GRACE: What?

PHIL: It's just.... They keep promoting me.

GRACE: Promoting you.

PHIL: Yeah. Raises, bigger office, perks.

GRACE: The bastards.

PHIL: The more they promote me, the tougher they need me to be. At first it's following rotten orders, then it's thinking up rotten ideas of your own. I've tried, I really have, but...I feel like I'm letting them down. Finally I go somewhere else.

GRACE: You're in personnel, and you think you can just go somewhere else? I'm in retail, I see what's going on. I used to spend my day saying, "Will there be anything else? Do you need some stockings to go with that?" Now I tell people, "I'm sorry, but the credit card company informs me that I must confiscate and destroy your card."

PHIL: Wow. What do they do?

GRACE: A lot of them try to grab it back.

PHIL: They come after you?

GRACE: It helps if you pick up the scissors before you tell them. Once you cut their name in two they kind of...deflate.

PHIL: I bet you could get another job.

GRACE: Jesus, Phil! This is what I'm trying to get through your skull! When a job like mine comes open, the line goes around the block! Don't you interview job applicants? Can't you see how desperate they are?

PHIL: They are at first, but I tell them their résumé looks good—and it does, their résumés all look amazingly good—I say we'll keep them in mind, and they cheer up.

GRACE: Oh. Don't ever do that. Phil, you shouldn't ever do that.

PHIL: Why not?

GRACE: You're getting their hopes up. You're not going to hire those people.

PHIL: We might.

GRACE: But you won't.

PHIL: We should.

GRACE: But you won't. Don't tell people something just to get their hopes up. It's a rotten thing to do. *(Pause)* The bathroom is this way?

PHIL: Yeah.

(As she goes, he wistfully picks up the mattress and drags it off. She turns and watches him as the lights crossfade to:)

Scene Five

(Daylight. They sit on the hood of the car. GRACE looks miserable. PHIL is eating a burger and watching her.)

PHIL: I wish you'd tell me why you're upset.

GRACE: What makes you think I'm upset? I've dropped the ball on a major commitment to Julia, I'm out a lot of money for a dress I never even wore, I'm lost, I'm standing in a parking lot in an overcoat and my underwear, I'm—sick.... You got some tissues?

PHIL: Somewhere in there.

(GRACE leans into the car and feels between the seat cushions. Her face crumples a bit and she sniffs loudly.)

PHIL: Are you crying?

GRACE: No.

PHIL: Are you sure?

GRACE: I have an allergy.

PHIL: To what?

GRACE: To people asking me a lot of questions when I'm crying.

(She grabs a hunk of red taffeta dress and blows her nose on that.)

PHIL: Is this 'cause we missed the wedding?

GRACE: I hate weddings. A wedding is designed to make the bride feel good about getting married by humiliating all the single women there. By the time she throws the bouquet, I don't want to catch the thing, I want to shoot it out of the sky. I'm sorry. I'll have a good cry and I'll be better in a minute or two.

PHIL: A good *cry*? A *good* cry? This is scaring the bejesus out of me. Can I do anything to help?

GRACE: *(Smiling a little)* You want to help me cry?

PHIL: I want to help you stop.

(GRACE *looks at him. She touches his face.*)

GRACE: You're a nice boy, Phil. You're a lot of fun.

(*Pause*)

PHIL: What do you want to do?

GRACE: Nothing.

PHIL: Where do you want to go?

GRACE: I don't care.

PHIL: Hey. Now you're talking. Hitting the road!

(PHIL *jumps in the car and guns the motor as* GRACE *climbs in.*)

PHIL: This is great, in a way.

GRACE: In what possible way is this great?

PHIL: It's almost as good as a road trip.

GRACE: What's a road trip?

PHIL: What. Is a *road trip*?

GRACE: Some kind of vacation?

PHIL: Vacation? No *way*. A vacation is valet parking and how much do we tip the maid.

GRACE: Those are bad things?

PHIL: A road trip is when you get in a car and see where you wind up. The great thing is not to know where you're going till you're just about there.

GRACE: How do you decide?

PHIL: You get an omen.

GRACE: An omen.

PHIL: Okay, we're driving along, taking likely looking roads—

GRACE: Likely looking?

PHIL: Say you're telling personal history stories, and up ahead you can turn onto, One: a freeway; or Two: a slow back road where you can see the moon. What's your choice?

GRACE: Back road?

PHIL: Exactly. But if you've got a Chuck Berry song on the radio?

GRACE: Freeway?

PHIL: That's it.

GRACE: You're going along, you're talking—

PHIL: Maybe you've got a game on the radio, junk food around your feet—junk food is very important—

GRACE: For energy?

PHIL: Atmosphere. I don't know—it only works if it's coming out of really garbagey circumstances.

GRACE: Game on the radio...

PHIL: Rock and roll, something. Okay, for instance: it's evening, you're driving through the outskirts of Indianapolis—this really happened—the sky's gone weird and it's affecting the radio reception, it's pulled in some sports roundup talk show, and they mention the Yankees are opening a home stand against the Red Sox the next day. And right that second, a line of businessmen gets off the bus ahead of you, all wearing pinstripe suits. What do you do?

GRACE: Pinstripes. The Yankees wear pinstripes.

PHIL: At home.

GRACE: You drive to New York.

PHIL: Yes! Yes! That is what you do! You drive all night, you take turns at the wheel, and sleep in the back seat. You get to the Bronx, you see the game, you drive back.

GRACE: You burn a lot of fossil fuel.

PHIL: You pull back into your street after a drive like that, you've done something.

GRACE: Something kind of goofy.

PHIL: Sure it's goofy, but what you've done is you know someone. You spend a few days with somebody in a space no bigger than this, you know who they are. You get a lot of thinking done.

(Pause)

GRACE: One: I have to buy some human clothing. Two: I need to be back for work tomorrow morning.

PHIL: Yes! Yes! You're gonna love this!

(PHIL races the engine. GRACE turns on the radio and searches the dial. He watches her.)

PHIL: Wow...

GRACE: What?

PHIL: You know what's great? Your back, between your shoulders. There's a curve.

GRACE: Watch the road.

PHIL: No, though, it's—your neck curves in, then out for your shoulders and then in again.

GRACE: I'm hunchbacked, you're saying.

PHIL: Bannh. Wrong. But *here's* what it is: that curve is because you have another set of curves that start at one shoulder and go across your shoulderblade and dip into your spine and out and up the shoulderblade on the other side and across that shoulder. So you've got these curves this way meeting across these curves running this other way. It's...harmonious.

GRACE: I feel like this *thing* now.

PHIL: You know, I could look at this back for a long time. *(A deep breath)* 'Cause I think what I'm trying to say is—

GRACE: Whoa. Slow down a sec.

PHIL: What?

GRACE: This...really isn't fair. Okay? You waltz around praising my body and wiping my nose and it isn't fair, so stop, okay? Please. Just stop.

PHIL: Stop what?

GRACE: You can't possibly keep this up. And right about the time I start getting used to all this...right when I start needing this...this...

PHIL: Well. Love, actually. And he says it!

(He honks the horn a few times.)

GRACE: Oh, this is bad.

PHIL: It's taken me the whole damn day!

GRACE: This is gonna be so bad.

PHIL: How are you feeling? You feeling any better?

GRACE: Wait a minute—are you saying you love me as a way of cheering me *up*?

PHIL: Doesn't it?

GRACE: You want to cheer someone up, you say, "There, there," you say, "Poor sweet baby." You don't make a life-changing announcement.

PHIL: Why not?

GRACE: Because "There, there" and "Poor sweet baby" don't *mean* anything. They're just noises people make. I worry that "I love you" is just this *noise* you're making.

PHIL: It's not.

GRACE: How do I know that?

PHIL: I'm telling you.

GRACE: Okay. I have to tell you something.

PHIL: Is this to do with why what I said didn't make you happy?

GRACE: *(Very unhappily)* I'm happy, Phil. It's scary, that's all. Anyway, yeah. It's some not necessarily really good news.

PHIL: I thought there was something on your mind. Anyway, I know all about it.

GRACE: What do you know?

PHIL: I got a call from Kyle. He told me he and Suzannah split up.

GRACE: My God.

PHIL: They haven't even gotten the credit card bills from the honeymoon.

GRACE: It's awful.

PHIL: Yeah, it is. But you're not Suzannah. Okay? I'm not Kyle. We're gonna be all right.

GRACE: Well, good. Good, I mean, I'm glad I didn't have to break it to you, that...really bad news, about...them. *(Pause)* I wonder.... Suzannah wanted to start a family right away. Boy, I wonder if she's pregnant.

PHIL: That would be pretty awful.

GRACE: You think so.

PHIL: Sure. What would she do?

(Pause)

GRACE: Basically she would have five options.

PHIL: Five—

GRACE: I'm just talking off the top of my head, here, but.... One: They split up for good and she has it and raises it alone—

PHIL: Can you picture that? "Son, this is your father. He and I were married for a couple of weeks a few years back." Unless she has a ton of money—

GRACE: *(To herself)* Strike one.

PHIL: Or an understanding family—

GRACE: *(To herself)* Swinging strike two.

PHIL: I wouldn't wish it on anyone.

GRACE: Two: She decides to have it and they stay together—

PHIL: Trapped and resentful.

GRACE: Rrright. Three: She decides not to have it—

PHIL: Which is of course her choice—

GRACE: For the moment, yes.

PHIL: But it's a sad thing to have to do, especially if she thinks she's running out of chances, I mean Suzannah must be, what—

GRACE: Thirty-four.

PHIL: Right.

GRACE: Four: They stay together, she has the abortion, and doesn't tell Kyle.

PHIL: That's her business. But what kind of marriage is that gonna be?

GRACE: Five: She doesn't have the baby and she doesn't have Kyle. Which leaves Suzannah with no good options.

PHIL: Poor Suzannah.

GRACE: Poor old Suzannah.

PHIL: You've given this a lot of thought, huh.

GRACE: Yeah.

PHIL: How come?

(Pause)

GRACE: Well. Even when you use protection, there's a danger. *(Pause)* And I was late this month. *(Pause)* So I thought I'd better see if I was pregnant. *(Pause)* But I'm not.

PHIL: Hunh.

(Blackout)

END OF ACT ONE

ACT TWO

Scene One

(PHIL *is driving. He's wearing cheap jeans, t-shirt, and sneakers, and a Minnesota Twins cap.* GRACE *is asleep in the back, out of sight.*)

PHIL: Grace? You awake? Hey, Grace?

(PHIL *turns on the radio. He flips through the static along the dial until he finds the song from the top of the show. The rhythm is a deep pounding and a higher, faster sound.* PHIL *listens and taps the steering wheel. Then the vocal to the song comes in. The words are spoken. The voices are* GRACE'S *and* PHIL'S.)

GRACE: *(On the radio)* So I thought I'd better see if I was pregnant.

(PHIL *stares at the radio.*)

GRACE: I'd bet I'd bet I'd better see if I was pregnant.

(PHIL *glances into the back seat and then back at the radio.*)

GRACE: I thought I'd better see if I was pregnant. But I'm not.

PHIL: *(On the radio)* Hunh!

GRACE: Even when you use protection, there's a danger. There's a a a a danger. I thought I'd better see if I was pregnant.

PHIL: *(On the radio)* Grace! We're running late!

GRACE: I was late this month.

(PHIL *mouths the words with the radio, increasingly stunned.*)

GRACE: I was laaaaate this, late this month. I thought I'd better see if I was pregnant. But I'm not.

(PHIL *turns off the radio.*)

PHIL: Grace?

(GRACE, *very pregnant, lies on a towel in the sun, wearing nothing but a baseball jersey, shades, and nasty high heels. She's smoking a cigarette elaborately. Bad girl stuff.*)

GRACE: What is it, Phil?

PHIL: Who is he?

GRACE: Who's who?

PHIL: Whose baby is it? Is it mine?

GRACE: If you think it's yours, it's yours.

PHIL: Whose is it really?

GRACE: I told you. Come on, there's a chance it's yours.

PHIL: Grace, please.

GRACE: Don't get mad?

PHIL: I never get mad.

GRACE: Okay, it was Harmon Killebrew.

PHIL: No. When? Where?

GRACE: Fantasy Camp. Phil, it had nothing to do with you. It's just—Harmon is bigger than you, and stronger than you, and richer than you, and older than you.

PHIL: Way older than me.

GRACE: Still swings from the hips, though. Phil, he's a Hall of Famer.

PHIL: Why did it have to be Killebrew? He was my idol.

GRACE: I don't know, it was dark. It might have been Rod Carew.

(Blackout)

Scene Two

(Engines roar. The wind blows. Traffic whizzes by. On the passenger side, GRACE opens her eyes and stretches. She is dressed the same as PHIL.)

GRACE: Where are we?

PHIL: I'm not looking at the map, I'm squinching up my eyes so I can't see the signs, and I won't ask for directions.

GRACE: Those are the rules?

PHIL: They're not rules, they're just part of the idea. A big point of a road trip is flexibility, Grace. *(Pause)* Hey, I told you I heard from my nieces and nephews?

GRACE: No, you didn't.

PHIL: Didn't I? Well, I did. My brother and sister both called and put the kids on to thank me for the Twins stuff I sent. Joshua thinks that because I live in Minneapolis, Kirby Puckett must be a friend of mine. What's great about being an uncle is I can say, "That's right, Josh, he is. Who do you think taught him to hit?" I mean, if I were his dad, I wouldn't say that kind of thing. Wouldn't be responsible. If I were his dad, I'd tell him the truth.

(Pause)

GRACE: Do you know where we're going yet? Seen anything omenish?

PHIL: Not yet.

GRACE: What time is it?

PHIL: I'm trying not to look at my watch.

GRACE: Why not?

PHIL: It's a road trip. There's no itinerary.

GRACE: Now entering—

PHIL: Don't tell me!

GRACE: Phil, why don't I drive, and then you can put a blindfold on. 'Cause I get the feeling I'm watching you kidnap yourself.

PHIL: I can look at the signs or I can look at the scenery. Tell you what. You search for omens. I don't care where we wind up.

GRACE: There's a tree! Tree, tree, orchard, forest, Forest Hills! We should go to Forest Hills! Or Ann Arbor...

PHIL: Try not to press it.

GRACE: Grain silos...long row of mailboxes...herbicide billboard...

PHIL: Relax.

GRACE: Are there times you never find it?

PHIL: I guess so. Sure.

GRACE: How long does it usually take?

PHIL: We may be passing omens galore and you're not in the frame of mind to see them.

GRACE: Now wait, you didn't tell me about a frame of mind.

PHIL: It won't work if there's too much in your head.

GRACE: I'm supposed to have nothing on my mind.

PHIL: *(Pointedly)* Yeah. Like if something's weighing on your mind? We might never get anywhere.

(Pause)

GRACE: Phil. What you said this morning.

PHIL: That I love you.

GRACE: *Oh*, man.

PHIL: It's still true.

GRACE: Really. Several hours later.

PHIL: I would love you no matter what.

GRACE: You shouldn't say that.

PHIL: Why not?

GRACE: I think you don't know what it means. When you say that to somebody—it's not a weather report, okay? It's supposed to be a promise. Would you promise me something, Phil? One favor.

PHIL: Anything. Anything. I promise.

GRACE: Ah, Phil. That's the thing. How am I supposed to trust you, when you think you can promise me anything?

(Pause. PHIL turns on the radio and begins scanning through the staticky dial. GRACE is watching him. The lights change, and the sound changes to flipping television channels.)

(PHIL leaves the car and waddles down to slump on a sofa bathed in blue television light. Between the light and his couch-potato posture, he looks awful. He's pointing a remote control.)

PHIL: It said 3:05. Four, no, five, no—Grace! Where's the *T V Guide*?

GRACE: In your lap.

PHIL: Aw, jeez. Get it for me, willya? Eleven, no, E S P N, no—*TV Guide* said Twins game 3:05.

GRACE: That's last week's, Phil.

PHIL: Shit. Maybe somebody else is playing. *(He holds down the "channel up" button on the remote control and we get little snatches of programs going by.)* Soap, soap, baby animals, soap, news, Oprah—

GRACE: Men who can't read a T V schedule, next on Oprah.

PHIL: Shut up! Huckleberry Hound, news, seventies made-for-T V movie, okay! Tire commercial! Gotta be a game.

GRACE: Phil? Where were you last night?

PHIL: Here we go. Jesus, wrestling! *(He holds down the remote button again.)* Courtroom drama, standup comedy, news, old movie, prevue guide, shopping network, stock market, infomercial, what is this—Geraldo, God on a stick, ancient sitcom, more God, don't know don't care, scramble channel, scramble channel, music video, scramble channel, music video, all right! Aerobics on the beach!

GRACE: Change it.

PHIL: I'm exercising here!

GRACE: Change it.

PHIL: Scramble, scramble, weather, Congress, Spanish soap, weather— God in heaven, two weather channels and no baseball— *Sesame Street.* We're back to the top, that's it. *(He turns off the set and stares out dumbly.)*

GRACE: Phil? Where were you?

PHIL: Hey! I don't ask where you go.

GRACE: I go to work.

PHIL: You wanted a kid. I said I'd always be there for you, and here I am, yes? Our deal was you work, I stay home with the baby. Yes?

GRACE: But, Phil—

PHIL: What?

GRACE: Phil? Where's the baby?

(Pause. PHIL thinks hard.)

GRACE: Phil?

PHIL: Hang on...

(Blackout)

Scene Three

(Engines, sunlight, wind. PHIL and GRACE in the car.)

GRACE: I want to thank you.

PHIL: For what?

GRACE: For this. The road trip. It's a good idea. You get a lot of thinking done.

PHIL: Hey.

GRACE: What?

PHIL: *(Pointing out the window)* Look at that. Oh, that is great.

GRACE: What?

PHIL: That. I love that.

GRACE: I don't even see what you're pointing at.

PHIL: The hillside above that farm. Those big red rocks—

GRACE: What about them?

PHIL: And the tips of whatever they've planted there—

GRACE: Wheat?

PHIL: Don't know, but—same red. See?

GRACE: Okay.

PHIL: Now look at the barn.

GRACE: Same red.

PHIL: I would do that. I would paint my barn in honor of those rocks and those plants. Look what they're doing!

GRACE: Maybe it didn't happen on purpose.

PHIL: Then there's a God.

GRACE: There's you, noticing.

PHIL: There he *is*! He's walking out of his house! Quick!

GRACE: What?

(He honks the horn.)

PHIL: In a red! Flannel! Shirt! Hold the wheel.

GRACE: What?

(PHIL lets go of the wheel and leans way out the window. GRACE yelps and grabs the steering wheel.)

GRACE: Phil! Jesus Christ!

PHIL: You! Farm guy! You are a great man! I want your autograph!

(PHIL sits back down and puts his hands on the wheel again. GRACE's fingers are frozen on the wheel. PHIL carefully pries them off. GRACE's hands reflexively grab for the dashboard.)

GRACE: Never ever ever ever—

PHIL: What's wrong?

GRACE: Scenery. I nearly died for scenery.

PHIL: *Great* scenery.

GRACE: Come on. In the winter, you think he paints the barn white? Does the chores in a dress shirt? Where have you *been*, Phil?

PHIL: *(Grinning)* All your life?

GRACE: All *yours. (Pause).* So that was our omen?

PHIL: That? No.

GRACE: Wasn't it?

PHIL: No. I just liked it.

GRACE: When you do find an omen, can I get a sense of what your reaction is going to be?

PHIL: It varies.

GRACE: I've hurt your feelings.

PHIL: It's okay.

GRACE: No, it's not okay. Because when I do it you tend to sulk.

PHIL: Sulk?

GRACE: You practically hold your breath till your face turns blue.

PHIL: I call that being tough. Living with my secret pain.

GRACE: When John Wayne does it, we call it being tough. John Wayne does not practically stick out his lower lip as if to say, "Look at me living with my secret pain." That we call sulking.

PHIL: I wish someone had told me that before. I get the feeling there's a lot of things people don't tell me. *(He looks at her.)*

GRACE: Watch the road. *(Pause)* Phil, it's hard to tell you the truth, sometimes. The truth about things is so vastly inferior to what you seem to think is going on. It's hard to spoil your fun.

PHIL: You make me sound like I'm some kind of kid.

(She just looks at him.)

PHIL: Ow.

GRACE: Phil, in this world there are lovable people and there are unlovable people. You, Phil, are frighteningly lovable. You love the world and it loves you right back. You go through your day like a goddamn receiving line. "Hiya, Phil," say the plants. "Look over *here*, Phil!" say the rocks. "Hey, Phil," says the barn, "How's our boy?"

PHIL: But—that's how people talk to a baby.

GRACE: Well. Everybody loves a baby.

PHIL: But they don't take him seriously. Do they.

(Pause)

GRACE: So what do you want to do—

PHIL: When I grow up? Hang out with you.

GRACE: How long?

PHIL: Indefinitely.

GRACE: Yeah. That's the thing.

PHIL: What do you want? For yourself?

GRACE: To watch the Twins win the pennant.

PHIL: Seriously. I mean, I know you're serious. But besides that.
What do you picture?

GRACE: I'm thirty-four years old. I don't picture myself anymore.
I see other people and wish that I could have been them.

PHIL: Why? I don't—this is what I cannot *get* about you. You say things
that are so *sad*, about yourself, and—listen. You know what I love to do?

GRACE: Everything. Everything you do, you love to do.

PHIL: You've never seen me at work. I know you're supposed to have
ambitions, but I just don't do anything in a champion caliber way. But what
I love to do is to see great things. I don't need to do anything. I just love to
know. I think the only thing I do really well is cheer. When you know
something is really great, you can look at the people you're with and say,
"You know what's great? That right there." When I'm alone with you,
I always want to point and say, "You know what's great? That woman
there." But the only other person in the room is booing all the time.
Which can be hard. (*Pause*) This whole drive I've been looking at you and...
doing that thing you said.

GRACE: What thing?

PHIL: I've been seeing all the times we've been together. I've never done this
before in my life. I know I haven't loved you very long. But I think I love
you in a lot of detail.

GRACE: Phil. The way you've been—seeing me today. There's a down side.
When you—if you fall out of love, if it's bad, you—when you look at
yourself—you see that awful time. And you have to be able to look at
yourself again.... So you lose that part of your life.

PHIL: This happened to you.

GRACE: Ages twenty-three through twenty-seven inclusive. Pretty much
gone. Meeting, courtship, marriage, divorce. Dim shapes, that's it.

PHIL: You've been married. You never told me.

GRACE: Not much left to tell.

PHIL: What was his name?

GRACE: Roy. His name was Roy. Is Roy, I guess, somewhere. Roy.
I haven't said his name in years. Roy. What a dumb name.

PHIL: You really don't remember anything?

GRACE: I remember the facts, but...I can't feel it. I remember his nose.
And...a fight we had in a café, he grabbed my arm. And standing on the
platform in the cold, his train coming around the corner, the rails and the
electric wires turning into lines of light, closer and closer, and then this
blinding light, like if the moon were as bright as the sun, and he walked out
of it. He had a big down coat, it squished when I hugged him. That's about
it.

PHIL: You had a whole marriage before you were the age I am now.

GRACE: Phil. I have never been the age you are now.

PHIL: Maybe you were and you don't remember.

GRACE: Yeah. I'd hate to see that happen to...someone I cared about. *(Pause)*
Pull over?

PHIL: Why?

GRACE: You heard me.

(The motor stops. Crickets. Starlight.)

PHIL: Now what?

(GRACE kisses him hungrily.)

PHIL: Umph!

(Her hands are all over him and he responds in kind.)

PHIL: Wow. Watch out for the— *(The horn honks.)* We could move to the
back, if you—

*(The horn honks. And again. And again, in a faster and faster rhythm.
The horn sound holds, and fades.)*

Scene Four

*(Darkness, lights, engine, wind. PHIL is driving. He is nodding a little.
On the passenger side, GRACE opens her eyes and stretches.)*

GRACE: Hi.

PHIL: Hi.

GRACE: Where are we?

PHIL: I don't know.

GRACE: What time is it?

PHIL: I bet this is a dumb question. Right in front of us, is there a gigantic black bat guiding us down the road?

(GRACE *looks. Pause.*)

GRACE: Yes there is.

PHIL: Thought so. The tips of its wings are touching the wheels?

GRACE: Yup. Gliding.

PHIL: The moon's behind us. It's the shadow of the car.

GRACE: Looks more like a bat.

(*He is shaking his head to stay awake.*)

GRACE: Think we need to rest?

PHIL: I'm okay.

(*Pause*)

GRACE: That was something back there.

PHIL: It was great.

GRACE: Yes it was. Listen. If I tell you something, will you try to remember it later?

PHIL: Sure.

GRACE: You are the most wonderful lover.

PHIL: You are, too.

GRACE: Just—remember I said so. (*Pause*) I have to tell you something.

PHIL: Great.

GRACE: No. Once we get home. I think it would be better if you didn't see me anymore.

PHIL: What?

GRACE: I could have waited till we got back, I mean I know this is going to make the rest of the drive kind of long, or we could have gotten back and I'd start waiting longer and longer to return your phone calls and see if it sort of dried up on its own. But I didn't, because I want to make sure that you know that this isn't about you. You are a treasure. Okay? It's me. I can't—you love to do so many things, but I have to start thinking about—other things—that—

PHIL: Like what? What things?

GRACE: I don't know!

PHIL: You do. You won't tell me.

GRACE: I know you. It would be so easy for me—God!—to hear you make a lot of promises right now. But I can't.

PHIL: I did something. I went wrong somewhere.

GRACE: No.

PHIL: I must have. It's because I'm younger than you.

GRACE: Phil, I just—I couldn't bear to go through life being the person who always tells you "No."

PHIL: This is not what—I drove all this way—

GRACE: We'd better go home.

PHIL: No.

GRACE: I knew I couldn't do this without hurting somebody, and now I have, so let's just go home, okay?

PHIL: No.

GRACE: What do you mean, "No"?

PHIL: I can't.

GRACE: Why not?

PHIL: I'm scared.

GRACE: Don't be scared.

PHIL: If I drive home I don't see you again.

GRACE: Phil.

PHIL: So I don't want to go home anymore.

GRACE: I *have* to say this, I don't want to, but—I have to get back in time for work. Okay?

PHIL: Maybe. I don't know. Maybe we're blowing off work today.

GRACE: I can't do that.

PHIL: I'm never going to see you again and you want to go to work?

GRACE: It's necessary.

PHIL: It's money. This is love. Listen.

GRACE: Sweet baby, this isn't a credit card commercial. This is me needing to keep my medical insurance. The rules of life don't screech to a halt because we love each other.

PHIL: They should.

GRACE: Yes. They should. But they won't. And I *can't*.... Having to tell you stuff like this is going to break my heart.

PHIL: I love you.

GRACE: I love you, too. Now drive me home.

(PHIL *shakes his head.*)

GRACE: Phil. You want to drive away from your responsibilities. That's great, you do that. But I cannot come along.

(*He looks at her.*)

GRACE: Watch the road.

(*He keeps looking at her.*)

PHIL: If you were a thousand miles away and my credit was gone and my money was gone and I couldn't rent a car or take a bus or hitchhike or borrow a car because I had no job and my friends would all have forgotten my name, I would walk all the way to you in my shoes and if I didn't have my shoes then I would walk it barefoot, because *that* I think is my responsibility.

(*He turns toward the road. Pause.*)

GRACE: You've been driving all night, haven't you?

PHIL: We needed to get away.

GRACE: We can't keep going like this forever. Eventually we're going to reach the ocean.

PHIL: We can sit on the beach. I'll watch you get a tan.

(*Snow begins to fall.*)

GRACE: Too much sun is bad for you.

PHIL: I'll buy you a hat.

GRACE: Uh, Phil?

PHIL: Hm.

GRACE: Is that snow? Phil, I see snow falling on the car.

PHIL: Probably very light hail.

(GRACE *sticks an arm out the window.*)

GRACE: Not cold...

PHIL: Some kind of pollen?

(PHIL *is nodding again.*)

GRACE: (*Wicked Witch of the East voice*) Poppies...poppies...

(PHIL *opens his eyes with a jolt.*)

PHIL: Woof! Man!

GRACE: You okay?

PHIL: I had this dream.

GRACE: When?

PHIL: Just now.

GRACE: Pull over, Phil.

PHIL: I dreamt I was driving a car—

GRACE: Which is what you are doing, keep it in mind.

(GRACE *turns on the radio. Static, then, a big band dance tune. The lights change to the dance floor.* PHIL *opens the car door and starts to get out.* GRACE *yanks him back.*)

GRACE: Phil! What the hell are you doing!

PHIL: I—what?

GRACE: Stay in the car!

PHIL: Wo.

GRACE: What were you doing?

PHIL: I thought I was having another flashback.

GRACE: Phil, how's about I do some driving, huh?

PHIL: I'm okay now. Really. Got my second wind.

(*Blackout. Crazy headlights. A long screech. A metallic crunch.*)

Scene Five

(GRACE *is sitting on the ground near the car.* PHIL *is standing over her. Light from a streetlight through a chainlink fence.*)

GRACE: I'm fine.

PHIL: Stay sitting. You may be in shock.

GRACE: I swear to you I am absolutely fine.

PHIL: Lucky we didn't roll it.

GRACE: Are you okay?

PHIL: Couple of scratches getting out. No problem. I wonder where we are.

GRACE: Is there a sign?

PHIL: I'll go look. Something's got to say.

(PHIL *crosses away and peers into the darkness.* GRACE *furtively checks herself for blood.* PHIL *comes back into the light.*)

GRACE: So where'd we land?

PHIL: Louisville.

GRACE: Kentucky?

PHIL: I don't know. Probably a lot of Louisvilles around.

GRACE: If it's Kentucky, you know what that means?

PHIL: Home of the Louisville Slugger.

GRACE: Finest wood ever to strike a baseball. Wow. You did it. Excellent destination. Oh, my God.

PHIL: What?

GRACE: Before we crashed. You said the car was being guided.

PHIL: Right. Big flapping bat.

GRACE: Phil! A *bat* guided us to *Louisville.* You see? Granted, I mean, one is an animal and one is sporting equipment, but the *word*—

PHIL: Grace. I may have put too much emphasis on this omen thing.

GRACE: But you see?

PHIL: We had an accident, that's all.

GRACE: We had an accident. An accident. Oh, God.

PHIL: What?

GRACE: You're right, I was wrong about the bat stuff. It's this. We've had an accident. Oh, Phil. Oh, jeez.

(*He holds her and rocks her on the ground.*)

PHIL: I know. It's okay. We've had a little accident. I know.

(*She looks at him.*)

GRACE: You do know.

PHIL: Well, jeez, Grace, I drive a thousand miles waiting for you to tell me something. There's not a lot of things it's gonna be.

GRACE: Give the boy a cigar.

PHIL: What, uh... What confused me, see, was that you'd said you weren't pregnant.

GRACE: I guess I did that, yeah.

PHIL: I kept waiting for you to tell me. I kept trying to help you tell me.

GRACE: Yeah. I figured that out.

PHIL: You could see what I was doing. And you still couldn't tell me. My whole life, I say, "You know what's great? You know what I love?" Anything I can think of to say, everybody knows it. So I'm this idiot.

GRACE: No, Phil—

PHIL: First time you talked I said, "Finally. Finally. Someone who will tell me anything." The good, the bad, if it's true I want it. My whole life. This shit. *(He turns away and cries.)*

GRACE: Phil. Poor sweet boy.

(He turns on her.)

PHIL: *Stop.* Calling me that. *(Pause)* How long.

GRACE: About four weeks.

PHIL: Four—

GRACE: Two weeks I didn't know. One week I wasn't sure. One week I was too scared to know. Phil, I was so scared I didn't even want to take the test. I took it today.

PHIL: A *month* you've been thinking about it. Never a word. That *shit* about Suzannah being pregnant. What was that?

GRACE: A trial balloon? I was looking for a way to—

PHIL: A month. Now I'm gonna think about everything that happened this month.

GRACE: Hey. You really wanted to help me out, why didn't you call me on it? Huh? Do you know what I've been going through?

PHIL: No. You didn't tell me.

GRACE: Because I was scared to death of what you'd do if you knew.

PHIL: Is it somebody else's?

GRACE: What?

PHIL: Is it?

GRACE: Who else's could it be?

PHIL: I don't know. I guess I don't know much.

GRACE: Are you accusing me of seeing someone else?

PHIL: You've been hiding one important thing, maybe you're hiding another one.

GRACE: What do you think I am?

PHIL: You're a liar.

GRACE: I didn't lie, I concealed something I didn't think you were ready to hear. Sometimes you have to do that when you're talking to a child.

PHIL: Cut it out!

GRACE: Why should I have told you? What good was it going to do me? I'm trying to figure out whether to change my whole life around and you're going, "Mo-om, Grace gots my baby and she won't share it with me! It's not fai-air!"

PHIL: You really are a bitch, Grace.

GRACE: Finally figured that out, huh?

PHIL: I was right. It is somebody else's child. Is that what you want? Fine. It's one hundred percent your child. God help it.

GRACE: You—

PHIL: Someone gives you his heart, you treat him like he's holding a piece of shit! You'll make a *great* mother, yeah!

GRACE: Never. *Ever.* Tell me I shouldn't be a mother. You of *all* people! How dare you tell me a child of mine needs God's help or anybody's help? What do you think a mother is, Phil, a nice warm lap? It's shitloads of stamina and blood in your eye and anything else it needs, you've got to be there and be there and be there. It's not fun. It's not a romance. It's love. I've waited half my life to do this and I put it off and put it off waiting till I turned into warm and fuzzy Mamma, well fuck that and fuck you, if I want a baby I'll have a baby and *raise* it and anybody tries to come between us, oh, God help 'em!

(*They stand there and stare at each other, too afraid to move. Long pause.*)

PHIL: I bet the car still runs.

GRACE: What? I didn't—

PHIL: The car. It should get us back.

GRACE: Give me the keys.

PHIL: No, I can—

GRACE: Get some sleep.

(*He takes the keys from his pocket and crosses to hand them to her. They trudge to the car and get in. GRACE starts the car and drives. Long pause.*)

PHIL: Listen. Whatever you decide. Would it help if we moved in together?

GRACE: What?

PHIL: I've been running some figures in my head, kind of a rough budget, and I think we could save maybe twenty percent off our combined expenses now. We could get a bigger place for less than we pay for two little ones, plus phone, plus utilities, and then food, big saving there, plus we could commute together, save on gas, parking—

GRACE: Commute together.

PHIL: Yeah. Couldn't we?

GRACE: To work.

PHIL: Oh. Well, yeah. My company doesn't have parental leave. We should, but we don't. *(He yawns deeply.)* I ought to talk to Jack my boss about that.

GRACE: Get some sleep.

PHIL: Think about it though?

(She nods. PHIL climbs into the back seat and curls up. Engine. Lights. Howling wind. GRACE adjusts the rear view mirror and looks back at PHIL. Softly, a baby begins to cry. GRACE listens. PHIL sits up sleepily and kisses her on the cheek.)

PHIL: It's okay, I'll go.

(GRACE watches PHIL leave the car and cross downstage. He has a baseball glove on one hand, with a baseball in the pocket.)

PHIL: Hey. Hey, pal. *(He kneels and speaks at baby height.)* Look—buddy, look at this. This is a baseball glove. It goes on your hand. *(He holds it out.)* You wear it to catch a baseball. *(He drops the baseball out of the pocket into his other hand.)* Pal. This is a baseball. A special baseball. *(He holds the ball and turns it over.)* You see this mark? Dan Gladden left that mark when he hit this ball with a baseball bat. He hit it so hard that it flew all the way up to a box in the sky where your Mom and I were watching. You see this here? He signed this ball. See? Dan. Gladden. This is for you, pal. *(He puts the ball back in the glove.)* These are yours.

(GRACE watches PHIL as he waits and listens until the sobbing fades away. Lights down on PHIL.)

(GRACE begins picking up speed. She smiles. The car is going faster and faster as the lights fade.)

Scene Six

(The car, in noonday sunlight. No one visible. Then PHIL's *arms stretch luxuriantly up from the passenger side.)*

PHIL: Mmmm. *(Pause.* PHIL *sits bolt upright, feeling frantically in front of him with his hands.)* Mngah! *(*PHIL's *left hand finds the steering wheel, to his left. He looks. He is not driving.)* Grace? *(She's not in the car.* PHIL *opens the door and puts out a tentative toe. Yes, the car is really stopped. He gets out of the car and looks around.)* Grace? *(He looks around, baffled.)* Where the hell am I?

*(*GRACE *enters, still wearing her road clothes, thoroughly dazed. She carries a cassette tape. He looks up and sees her.)*

PHIL: Where'd you go?

GRACE: Didn't want to wake you... *(She leans on the hood of the car.)*

PHIL: What time is it?

GRACE: I don't know...

PHIL: Where are we?

GRACE: I'm going to say something...

PHIL: I'm not very awake here.

GRACE: I'm gonna have the baby.

*(*PHIL *stands up fast.)*

GRACE: Quick! What are you thinking!

PHIL: Uh.

GRACE: Right now! Don't sugarcoat it!

PHIL: Rookie from the country!

GRACE: What?

PHIL: Rookie from the country. Grace, you're gonna—

GRACE: What rookie from the country?

PHIL: All of them, you know.

GRACE: No, I don't.

PHIL: Old-time ballplayer story—boy's never seen the city, big club calls him up, you know, that one.

GRACE: This is what you're thinking.

PHIL: Very first picture, swear to God. The rookie tells a cab driver to take him to the ballpark, and they pull up outside the biggest damn building he's ever seen. He walks inside the walls. And far away, he sees a diamond. The team is taking batting practice, the rookie can see stars he's only dreamed about, hearing games late at night on the radio. He starts to walk toward them, to tell them he's here, he's finally here.

GRACE: And a guard walks up to throw him out.

PHIL: Yes! Always!

GRACE: And the guard says, "What do you think you're doing?"

PHIL: And the rookie says, "This is where I'm gonna play ball."

GRACE: And the guard says, "I bet you think you're pretty good."

PHIL: And the rookie looks at his team. And he says, "Yeah."

(Pause)

GRACE: I *love* that story. That is *great*.

PHIL: Can I tell you something? I've never told this to anyone.

GRACE: Go ahead.

PHIL: Lots of times... Lots of times I don't even *like* baseball.

GRACE: What?

PHIL: Come on, admit it, the game is slow. Nothing much happens. By July the season feels like it'll never get done, and they're still only halfway home. Look, when I was five years old the Twins won the division. Got swept by the Orioles in the playoffs. Broke my heart. The next year they finished twenty-six and a half games out of first. But every night I listened to the games. Every morning I read the box scores. I never stopped going to the park. In '87 they were the World Champions. Last year they were dead last. I never stopped rooting.

GRACE: What are you trying to say?

PHIL: Grace, I'm a baseball fan. I know how to make a commitment.

GRACE: Phil. It's only a game.

PHIL: Right. It's only a *game*. And I've been following that every day for twenty-one years. You would be my *family*.

(GRACE's face crumples a bit.)

PHIL: You're crying.

GRACE: It's okay, Phil. It's a good cry. Does your tape player work?

PHIL: Yeah. There's a thing you have to do with a screwdriver.

(She holds out the cassette.)

GRACE: Come on.

(They get in the car, GRACE *in the driver's seat. She puts the tape in the tape deck.* PHIL *monkeys with it.)*

PHIL: So where are we?

GRACE: I found a clinic.

PHIL: Are you okay?

GRACE: They have this Mister Microphone thing they put against your tummy.

(A deep and rhythmic pounding, and another, softer and faster sound. It's the beat from the beginning of the first and second acts.)

PHIL: What is that?

GRACE: Heartbeats. Mine's the loud one.

PHIL: Wow.

(They listen for a while.)

PHIL: So where are we going?

GRACE: Well. Kids gonna take a little trip.

PHIL: I am?

GRACE: We are. Want to come?

(He nods vigorously. The engine roars, and the heartbeats fade into it.)

PHIL: So where're those Kids headed, Vin?

GRACE: Down the Mississippi, Red. The report is they're driving so fast the radar can't pick 'em up. Aaaand it looks like they're headed for Texas.

PHIL: Vin, it looks like they're California bound!

GRACE: They're headed for the beach. Red, they've got surfboards!

PHIL: They're paddling west!

GRACE: Kids' gonna see the world!

PHIL: There is nothing this Kid cannot do!

GRACE: Kid's landed in Asia and hit the ground running.

PHIL: Freeing Tibet singlehanded, Vin!

GRACE: The Kid cannot stop, just cannot stop!

PHIL: Finding everyone a homeland!

GRACE: Helping Europe make decent popular music!

PHIL: Vin, the Kid is raising the Titanic!

GRACE: Raising Babe Ruth from the dead—

PHIL: And trading him back to Boston!

GRACE: This Kid is *great*!

PHIL: Making Detroit build a really great roadster again!

GRACE: I *love* this Kid!

PHIL: The Kid is climbing into that car!

GRACE: He's turning on the radio!

PHIL: The World Series is on!

GRACE: And the Kid is at the plate!

PHIL: Here comes the pitch—

GRACE: The bases are loaded for the Kid—

PHIL: He swings!

GRACE: It's a towering drive!

PHIL: Lou Gehrig is running!

GRACE: Cool Papa Bell is running!

PHIL: Roberto Clemente is flying!

GRACE: The ball clears the fence!

PHIL: The ball leaves the park!

GRACE: As it goes out of sight it is rising...

PHIL: The Kid rounds the bases and heads for home...

GRACE: And the Kid...

PHIL: The Kid has a heartbeat.

(PHIL *holds up one hand.* GRACE *slaps her own into it. They clasp hands.*)

PHIL: Jeez, I love you.

GRACE: I love you so much.

(*They kiss.*)

GRACE: Phil.

(*The kiss goes on.*)

GRACE: Phil, there's something else.

PHIL: Something *else*?

GRACE: When the doctor listened to the microphone thing she heard something funny and she did a test to be sure.

PHIL: Oh my God. Is it healthy? Is it all right?

GRACE: They're fine.

PHIL: They're—

(Pause)

GRACE: It's twins.

PHIL: You're kidding. It's twins?

GRACE: We got a bonus baby.

PHIL: It's TWINS?

GRACE: It's an omen.

PHIL: Wow. Hey, you know what's great?

GRACE: Yeah.

(GRACE and PHIL smile at each other. Heartbeats and music. The lights fade.)

END OF PLAY

SHOW AND TELL

SHOW AND TELL was commissioned by South Coast Repertory. It was presented by South Coast Repertory as a workshop directed by Lisa Peterson; in the Playwrights' Center's 1991 Midwest Playlabs as a workshop directed by William Partlan; and in readings by Upstart Stage, the Playwrights' Center, and New Dramatists.

The world premiere of SHOW AND TELL was presented on 6 November 1992 by the Repertory Theatre of St Louis, Steven Woolf, Artistic Director, Mark D Bernstein, Managing Director. The company was:

COREY	Susan Erickson
SETH	Jim Abele
IRIS/LUCY	Mickey Hartnett
ANN/GAIL	Kim Sebastian
SHARON/ERINN	Brenda Denmark
FARSTED	R Ward Duffy
Director	Susan Gregg
Set and lights	Max De Volder
Costumes	J Bruce Summers
Music and sound	Stephen Burns Kessler
Stage manager	Champe Leary

ACKNOWLEDGMENTS

In addition to those named above, I am especially indebted to David Emmes, Martin Benson, Jerry Patch, and John Glore at South Coast Repertory; Dennis Barnett, Carter Lewis, and Julian López-Morillas at Upstart Stage; David Moore and Jeffrey Hatcher at the Playwrights' Center; and Anne Bogart at New Dramatists for their help with SHOW AND TELL.

My thanks also to the National Endowment for the Arts, the Jerome Foundation, and the Playwrights' Center for their generous financial support during the writing of the script.

CHARACTERS

COREY, early thirties, a schoolteacher
SETH, late thirties, a government man
FARSTED, late twenties, a working man
IRIS, fifties, a coroner
LUCY, fifties, a grandmother
SHARON, forties, a forensic investigator
ERINN, forties, a mother
ANN, twenties, an administrative assistant
GAIL, twenties, a mother

IRIS doubles with LUCY, SHARON with ERINN, ANN with GAIL. These three women are a presence on the stage during some scenes in which their characters do not appear, as noted.

SET

A wooden institutional table and four wooden chairs. An open space. A door through which the entrances are made.

ACT ONE

Scene One

(COREY stands downstage. She holds some postcards. There is a soft hissing sound.)

COREY: In Show and Tell, we find an object we can learn from. We learn who it belongs to and how they use it. Always remember to ask for permission before you bring anything in. *(Three quiet knocks, as if on a door)* Some objects are toys, or tools. The ones I've brought today are souvenirs. A souvenir is a tool for your memory. *(Three quiet knocks)* These are pictures I brought back from a trip I took a long time ago. I'll pass them around in a minute. They're pictures of the capital city. Who can tell us the name of the capital city? That's right. *(She looks at a postcard.)* Here's what the city looks like when you're flying through the air. See all the big white buildings? *(She looks at a postcard.)* This is the Capitol building at night. See the dome on top, all lit up? At night in the city, the lights are so shiny they drown out the stars. The sky is as dark as the land is here. But the streets are so bright, you feel like you're walking through the starry sky. *(She looks at a postcard.)* This is my favorite building: the art museum. The museum is filled with rooms, and every single room is filled with pictures. Do you want to paint pictures later today? Good. *(She looks at a picture in a little frame.)* The last one is a picture that I bought in the museum. It's a picture of a real picture in another museum, and it's really spooky, see, there's a knight on a beautiful horse, and his little dog, and the knight is talking to a skeleton. Some pictures are of animals or people or nature scenes. This is a picture of an idea. *(Three quiet knocks)* Those are my objects. You can learn so much about people by sharing their possessions. We share them and it's like sharing the people we care about. *(Three quiet knocks)* We show that we care by learning. *(Three quiet knocks)* That's what we do in Show and Tell.

(Four louder knocks. Lights down on COREY.)

Scene Two

(SETH *is standing contemplating a spot on the fourth wall at slightly above eye height.*)

SETH: Iris.

IRIS: What is it, Seth?

SETH: Look at this.

IRIS: What?

SETH: Clear through the wall.

IRIS: It's not—

SETH: Look.

IRIS: Tibia?

SETH: Femur, my guess. Children, remember.

IRIS: Terrible.

SETH: Senseless tragedy. But clear through the wall! Physics, boy... Bring the staff in, show them this. Why did no one see this before?

IRIS: We didn't think to look. Clear through—

SETH: When everyone has seen it, get it downstairs with the rest.

IRIS: It's a mess down there. I think we may be looking at a mass grave situation.

(ANN *enters.*)

ANN: Seth? Excuse me? Someone named Sharon says—

IRIS: Sharon's on this one?

ANN: She says—she has arrived and would like to see you.

SETH: Is she on the phone?

(SHARON *enters.*)

SHARON: Live! Live and in person! The message I gave this girl was to tell you to open that door or I'd blow your house in! Gimme some!

(SHARON *throws her arms around* SETH.)

SETH: How about this. Together again.

SHARON: Iris! I see you over there. Keeping an eye on this boy?

IRIS: Sharon. Good to see you.

(Everyone sits around the table.)

SETH: Are we up to speed? Sharon?

SHARON: I just got here. I've got a fairly reliable list of the victims, I've had a glance at the physical evidence, I've done a little interviewing. This, forgive me, is one pathetic bunch of survivors. It's time to ask: Is it my imagination or is grief always very tiresome?

IRIS: Never lose your curiosity.

SHARON: I've got it in storage somewhere.

SETH: Good work. Ann?

ANN: We've taken over the school building. The local authorities have the east wing as a communications center. We've pushed the press in there as well.

SETH: Good. They can keep each other company and we'll get our work done. Ann, this is your particular brief. I'll update the press mornings and afternoons, and immediately upon breakthroughs. In exchange, everybody stays where they've been put. Clear?

ANN: Clear.

SETH: People, about the press. Close-order drill. No exclusives, no leaked photographs, and no swarming over the bereaved. All statements coordinated through me. "The governor has committed every resource to ascertaining causes and releasing remains as quickly as possible. We have excellent cooperation from local law enforcement. No one has claimed responsibility, we're ruling nothing out." Ann?

ANN: We put the parents in the west wing. Some are under sedation and we have a room and local medics for them.

SETH: How many grief counselors do we have?

ANN: Ah. Well. There was a carload of them coming up from the city, but their car slid off the road.

SHARON: I love it! The ambulance chases them for a change!

ANN: They're being examined and treated.

SETH: And are helping each other work through the experience, no doubt. Let people know we'll have to take up the slack there for a while.

ANN: There's a room set up for Sharon's forensic work. Iris and the assistant coroners have the victims in the basement.

SETH: Where are the witnesses?

ANN: There were no witnesses per se, everyone in the room was killed.

SHARON: Their teacher was just outside. She was the first one in.

SETH: Where is she?

ANN: I don't know. I've been handling things here.

SHARON: I think I've seen her a couple of places.

SETH: What is she, wandering from room to room? How is she?

SHARON: We got a basic statement....

SETH: Ann, have her found and put her somewhere. Good work.

(ANN *exits.*)

SETH: Iris?

IRIS: It's a jigsaw puzzle down there. Very few edge pieces.

SHARON: Oy oy oy. Mass grave?

SETH: No. I don't think a mass grave will suffice.

IRIS: Are you asking me to sew name tags onto all of them?

SHARON: Seth! Show everyone a little mercy, huh?

IRIS: You know how much time that would take? I could lose myself in a problem like this for weeks.

SHARON: Weeks? Jesus.

IRIS: You know how I get, down there in the cold rooms.

SETH: I will not tell the peasantry we think of their dead children as an undifferentiated mass. It sends a bad message.

SHARON: Think of what it'll put the families through. They'll start asking themselves why their children are so hard to recognize. They'll try not to picture it, but they will.

SETH: And if we give them a mass grave? What'll they picture then? Their children asleep in each others' arms?

(FARSTED *enters with* ANN *close behind.*)

FARSTED: Excuse me.

ANN: Mr Farsted. If you could just wait out—

FARSTED: Sir?

IRIS: Ann? Who is this?

ANN: I'm sorry. His son—

IRIS: One of the—?

FARSTED: I'm looking for my boy.

ANN: Didn't the sheriff's office sit everyone down this morning?

FARSTED: I had work. I just need to know what—

ANN: There's a room where you can wait—

FARSTED: I'm looking for the room where I can get my boy and go home. Where's that room at?

SHARON: Mr—

FARSTED: Farsted, Ma'am.

SHARON: Mr Farsted, some people behave as if grief gave them license to act badly. You're not like that, are you?

FARSTED: But—

ANN: Mr Farsted, if you'd come with me—

FARSTED: Don't I have a right to get my son back? If I have to sign something, I'll sign. I can prove he's mine. I know the government has its own way of doing things. If I need to pay someone, for a permit, a little compensation for your trouble, I'll do it. Name your price. My wife—

SETH: Where is your wife?

FARSTED: They have her in a room where she has to lie down.

SETH: Mr Farsted. First of all, let me express that I cannot possibly feel the depth of your loss. Secondly, I am speaking to you with the utmost frankness. I expect you to be discreet with what I tell you.

FARSTED: Thank you, sir.

SETH: You needn't call me sir. Were you in the service?

FARSTED: In peacetime.

SETH: Nonetheless, you know what an explosion can do. If I tell you there was a massive explosion at very close quarters, you know what that means.

FARSTED: They're hard to identify. The bodies.

IRIS: If it were even that simple.

SHARON: You have to understand: When death comes like this it leaves almost nothing intact.

SETH: That's how we know they died instantly.

FARSTED: Really?

SETH: No question. Now looking at your son and the other children will help us learn the cause.

FARSTED: His momma keeps asking for him.

SETH: Mr Farsted, what made him your son is not downstairs.

FARSTED: I want what's left. A box with his name on it, anything at all, she keeps asking and asking and somebody has to stop her, I can't make her stop, I can't force her to, I mean you'd have to be an animal.

SETH: We shall identify the dead, and we shall place the blame. We have been sent here to name the names, and we shall not rest until we do. Will that satisfy you?

FARSTED: Yes, sir. Thank you, sir.

ANN: This way, Mr Farsted.

(ANN *shows* FARSTED *out and is about to follow.*)

SETH: Ann. In the future, have the door more carefully watched. Please.

ANN: Yes, Seth. I'm very sorry. *(She exits.)*

IRIS: Merciful God.

SHARON: Aren't you happy in your job, Seth? Don't you welcome each new day?

IRIS: Are you willing to endure weeks of that?

SETH: If we leave them a mass grave, they'll have to endure it forever. You heard the man. They need something with the name of what they loved.

IRIS: They will not get what they loved. What they will get, if they insist on getting something, will be a few human parts, inevitably mixed with a certain amount of desk and textbook and so on.

SETH: Give them anything they can bury.

IRIS: I will not misidentify remains.

SHARON: You're both right, okay? You're both too fair for this world, okay? Now. Iris, start piecing them together. Don't worry about the names yet. Seth promised, you gonna make a liar out of him? Huh?

IRIS: All right.

SHARON: You're a champ. Seth, people care about you. Take it into account. Now make a statement. Don't say they're unidentifiable. Say we need the remains for the investigation. When they start screaming, blame it on me.

SETH: Sharon, I couldn't ask you to—

IRIS: I'll try and see that it doesn't come to that.

SHARON: Christ, the time you people waste being right.

IRIS: Off we go. (IRIS *exits.*)

SHARON: Already we've got a fight. You're not making this any easier.

SETH: It's not supposed to be easy.

SHARON: Can I give you some advice? An event this bad, you bundle it up neat and you get the hell away. I'm doing my job, okay? But I am nothing here but cameras and tweezers and little plastic bags.

SETH: Have I asked for anything else?

SHARON: From me? No. From you, I don't know.

SETH: I'm just working.

SHARON: Good, because if you start feeling this one, kiddo, you will be gone gone gone. You hear me?

SETH: I hear you.

SHARON: Good. Now come on, let's go wading.

(SHARON *exits.* SETH *looks at the bone in the wall as the lights fade.*)

Scene Three

(COREY *stands holding an autoharp case. There are splatters of blood on her arms.* GAIL *is sitting at the table with her head down, sedated. Suddenly, as if a door had been opened onto the sound, a woman wails and sobs, "No, no, no, no," and is subdued.* LUCY *enters, carrying a shopping bag full of child's art. She turns back to call:*)

LUCY: Erinn! This must be the place!

(LUCY *sits near* GAIL *as* ERINN *enters.*)

LUCY: Gail, here you are, darling. Right, you just rest.

ERINN: *(Indicating* COREY*)* Lucy.

LUCY: Corey? How are you?

COREY: They wouldn't assign me to a classroom.

LUCY: My God. Rest, Corey.

ERINN: You of all people.

COREY: There has to be a lesson in this.

(*Offstage, a woman's voice begs, "No but I no but I no I have to have to have to...."*)

COREY: I'm fine. You're the ones.

(FARSTED *enters.*)

FARSTED: I spoke to the people in charge.

LUCY: Farsted, good for you. What's going to happen to the children?

FARSTED: These things have to be coordinated through a central authority. They're trying to learn the cause of it.

LUCY: I got here just as quick as I could. They called me up and said someone would need to identify them.

FARSTED: Now they're saying it could be a long time.

LUCY: I took everything off the refrigerator and stuffed it in a bag. Why did I do that?

ERINN: If you didn't put them in a bag they'd blow all over.

LUCY: Why bring them here? I must have had a reason.

FARSTED: The governor's man says they need the children for evidence about who did it.

LUCY: I can't believe someone meant this to happen.

ERINN: We have enemies. Not the town but I mean the state, or the country.

FARSTED: We stand for something.

ERINN: Some people are saying it's gangs.

FARSTED: Nah. Gangs? Not up here.

ERINN: Or a conspiracy.

LUCY: A conspiracy of who? Who's going to conspire against children?

FARSTED: They were our children. It could be against us.

LUCY: What have we done that anybody would conspire against us? We're not in charge of anything. What would be the point?

FARSTED: That's their thing—no point. So everybody's terrorized.

ERINN: They want everybody to be part of their war.

LUCY: This isn't a war. You know when you're in a war, you know it for a fact. Everyone has their duty to do. I was a girl, and by the end I was building munitions.

FARSTED: They won't let me do anything. Making me sit here and I've got jobs.

LUCY: In a war there are heroes all the time. You know their names.

ERINN: Farsted's father.

LUCY: More than our share. A lot of Gold Star mothers in this town. No. This was an accident. It has to be an accident.

FARSTED: Corey found them.

LUCY: Corey? Couldn't it have been an accident?

COREY: I don't know.

FARSTED: You didn't see who did it, did you?

COREY: No. Someone ought to know what I saw.

ERINN: Don't tell me.

LUCY: Me neither, for God's sake. I don't want to think of them like that.

ERINN: Think of how they've already arrived in paradise. Think of them in heaven.

(LUCY *takes artwork out of the bag.*)

LUCY: Corey, wasn't that funny last week when she brought me in to Show and Tell? Me telling the children about when irons were made of iron and we won the war? She'd bring home these paintings, I couldn't tell what they were supposed to be, she'd say, "Gran, it's *obviously* a *cow*," or whatever it was.

ERINN: The minute they learn something they think they must have been the first ever to hear it, so they go try and teach it to you. "You know what, Mom? And you know what?"

(GAIL *breathes with increasing struggle.*)

LUCY: What is this, now? What did she tell me? I'll never know.

COREY: Lucy. Gail's going into shock.

LUCY: Gail? Honey? Rest easy now.

ERINN: She's in God's hands even this day, honey.

COREY: Farsted. Pick her up and carry her to the next room. There's a clinic.

(FARSTED *lifts* GAIL *in his arms.*)

LUCY: Careful, Farsted.

FARSTED: Gail? Come on with me, baby. You've gained a bit since high school, huh? I've got you. We're gone.

(FARSTED *exits, carrying* GAIL.)

ERINN: This world is so dangerous now. Everything's going along and suddenly it'll all—explode. Not for us to know.

(LUCY *begins gathering pictures into a pile.*)

LUCY: This wasn't the wisest thing to do.

ERINN: Now isn't that a pretty one.

LUCY: Isn't it? She painted a multicolored background and covered it all with black crayon, see? That's a whole crayon's worth. And then she scraped away lines in the black to expose the color behind it. That's how it comes out looking this way, with the multicolored lines. See? You're so clever with them, Corey. How do you get all these ideas for arts and crafts?

COREY: We try to pin down a scene or a feeling, a part of our memory. We pin it down, even if we bend it a little, even if there's no real life left in the thing at all. But maybe it reminds us of a living time, maybe it reminds us that we saw the scene, we felt the feeling, we were there. Maybe that bent-up thing on the piece of paper becomes one of the ways we recognize ourselves.

(They are staring at her.)

COREY: Arts and crafts. That's what we do in arts and crafts.

(COREY exits.)

ERINN: Is she going to be all right? With children?

LUCY: Yes.

ERINN: Fine. I was asking a question and I have been answered.

LUCY: And she's right. Lord above. I brought these because they said they were identifying the children, so I brought something to identify my granddaughter. My granddaughter is the one who did these. Grief makes you stupid. That's wrong, somehow. Do you feel stupid?

ERINN: Sure. Nothing new.

LUCY: Here's one she painted with just a line of plain white glue. You see? I think it's supposed to be herself. All in glue and then she shook the sparkles onto the paper. She showed me how she'd done it, all over the paper, and then turned the paper upside down, and shook it. I think that was her favorite part, shaking it. And turned it right side up again, and the drawing was all sparkles. She brought me the painting the day she made it. Sparkles in her hair, in her clothes. She said they'd been rained on her by the painting. Her mother had to wash all the clothes she wore that day by themselves, or those sparkles would have gotten into everything. She can act so spoiled, that child. Well. All spoiled, now. Well. Well. *(She brushes at her clothes)* All over me now. *(Pause)* I know what you're asking. She's a good teacher, but I wonder what they were learning from her.

(The lights fade.)

Scene Four

(SETH *pores over photographs and charts at the table.* COREY *enters, carrying her autoharp case, and watches him for a moment.*)

COREY: I bet I'm not supposed to be here. I couldn't sit there anymore, lot of grieving people.

SETH: I thought everyone here was waiting for remains to be released.

COREY: No.

SETH: You're not a parent?

COREY: I'm a teacher.

SETH: A teacher.

COREY: Yeah, that's me. Corey. I've got information.

SETH: Yes?

COREY: I need some help with this information.

SETH: Didn't anyone talk to you?

COREY: Somebody asked me some questions, but I don't think they were the right ones. Who are you?

SETH: My name is Seth. I'm in charge. Ann!

COREY: Good, because I've got to get this out of my head a little, I can't share my head with it, there isn't any room for me, and I'm going to have to leave.

SETH: Stay here. Talk to me.

COREY: Okay, until I get to the bottom of this, after that I don't know.

(ANN *enters.*)

ANN: Oh, Jesus, I'm sorry. Ma'am, if you come with me—

SETH: Ann, could I have a damp cloth, please? Warm.

(ANN *exits.*)

SETH: Do you have any idea who did it?

COREY: No.

SETH: Do you know what kind of device may have caused it?

COREY: No.

SETH: Well. The kinds of evidence we're interested in at this point come either from objects or from eyewitness accounts.

COREY: But I was right there.

SETH: Very close.

COREY: I saw the whole thing.

SETH: The aftermath.

COREY: I should have been killed.

SETH: But you weren't.

(ANN *enters with a damp cloth, which she hands to* SETH.)

SETH: Thank you.

(ANN *exits.* SETH *begins to swab the blood from* COREY'*s forearms.*)

COREY: What are you doing?

SETH: You've got something on you. What are you carrying, there? That case.

COREY: Christ. This is an autoharp. Which I am carrying because the morning is supposed to start with music.

SETH: You've been carrying this around all day?

COREY: I left it in the teacher's lounge, and I told the children I'd go get it and be back in time for the bell. And I went there and got it and came back....

(SETH *holds the autoharp.*)

SETH: Corey. Your students are dead. They're all dead.

COREY: I saw.

(COREY *releases the autoharp, and* SETH *puts it on the table.*)

COREY: The door blew open, hit the wall, slammed back, shattered. I saw inside that doorframe for a fraction of a second and I remember thinking, "What's wrong with this picture?" It's a learning test, "What's wrong with this picture?" That's what we do, testing potential. I pulled the door free and went inside. Everything is wrong in this picture. Maybe you can help me, because they tell me school is closed, and if I can't learn something— my God, all my life—nursery school, elementary, secondary, high school, teachers college, student teacher, teacher—learning, up a grade, learning, up a grade, learning, if I can't do that...I need to learn why I'm not dead. Did the government send anyone here who can teach me why I'm not dead?

SETH: I'll try to find out.

COREY: The autoharp isn't much of an instrument. It's a handy instrument if you can't play an instrument, you just push the buttons for the chords. It

keeps them in tune. *(She demonstrates pushing imaginary chord buttons on the lid of the case, singing:)*
In C major's fair city
Where D minor's so pretty
I C major my eyes on sweet Molly Malone... *(Her voice trails off.)*
I'd have thought I'd be crying by now.

SETH: You don't want to cry?

COREY: No.

SETH: Do you want to sleep?

COREY: No no no.

SETH: Are you hungry?

COREY: Wouldn't food make me sick?

SETH: Think about it.

COREY: I'm not hungry.

SETH: Do you want to be alone?

COREY: I want—can you believe this? I'm chatting about what I want.

SETH: What do you want?

COREY: I just *want*. I've got such a want.

(ANN enters, carrying a plastic bag full of sharp metal shards.)

ANN: Seth?

SETH: Yes, Ann.

ANN: Sharon wants to know if you recognize this.

SETH: Corey, shall I have Ann take you over now—

COREY: No. Don't make me go back and sit with those parents.
I've been staring at their faces. Seeing their children's features. Ruined.

SETH: Stay here.

ANN: Seth?

SETH: Right. *(He studies the bag.)* Where'd she find this?

ANN: Sharon found it in the room, Iris found it in the bodies.

SETH: I've seen this stuff before. Where do I know this stuff?

ANN: You know this stuff?

SETH: This is one of ours. An old one. A couple of generations of weapon back. The shrapnel has a particular curl to the edges. It flies more wildly that way. It was someone's bright idea, it's the signature of this design. The characteristic ways it meets the body are documented in the literature. It did its job. I wonder who we gave it to.

COREY: Who could think of something like that?

SETH: Someone like me.

COREY: No. They must hate human life.

SETH: They can spot the flaws.

(SETH *writes on the bag as* SHARON *enters.*)

SHARON: *(To* ANN*)* There you are. Has the bomb squad finished searching?

ANN: Yes. They've done all the public buildings.

SETH: *(Holding the bag out to* SHARON*)* There's what you wanted to know.

SHARON: *(Taking the bag and handing him another, full of bits of brown stuff)* Great, I'll trade you. *(She reads his label.)* Yeah, I thought so. *(To* ANN*)* Did they turn up anything else?

ANN: No.

SETH: I want to know the minute someone claims responsibility. Thanks, Ann.

(ANN *exits.* SETH *examines the bag.*)

SETH: What is this?

SHARON: Bits of a mystery, thought you'd be interested. *(To* COREY*)* You're the teacher, right? Some kind of classroom thing? Science lesson?

COREY: I don't recognize it.

SETH: It's flesh.

SHARON: It's so old we weren't sure right away. At first we thought leather, but—

SETH: —leather doesn't have cartilage—

SHARON: Yeah. *(To* COREY:*)* Picture the room. Stuffed hamster? Mummified cat? Anything like that?

COREY: No. They've never given me money for science equipment. I spoke to the P T A.

SETH: I want this. All there is.

SHARON: There's lots of it, in little bits.

SETH: What distribution?

SHARON: Here.

(She hands him a diagram. They bend over it. COREY *tries to see, and can't. She wanders away, roaming the room.)*

SETH: It must have been very close to the epicenter.

SHARON: Look at the configuration.

*(*COREY *notices something on the wall.)*

SETH: Hm. What does it remind me of?

SHARON: I don't know.

COREY: Oh, my God. Oh, my God in heaven. I know what that is. That's a bone.

SETH: Clear through the wall.

SHARON: Ah, hell.

COREY: My God, my God, my God...

SETH: Ann!

SHARON: Terrible—

SETH: Senseless tragedy—

COREY: What would it *take*? To tear it off and then to...clear through the wall.

*(*ANN *enters.* COREY *has never taken her eyes off the bone.* SETH *has never taken his eyes off* COREY. SHARON *takes this in.)*

ANN: Seth? You called me?

SHARON: Tell Iris she forgot something, would you?

*(*ANN *exits.)*

SHARON: Seth. You want the rest of this stuff?

SETH: Yeah.

*(*SETH *puts the stuff back in the bag and hands it to* SHARON.*)*

SHARON: *(To* COREY:*)* You've got a sharp eye. Try not to call on God whenever you see something. He gets bored and stops listening. *(She exits.)*

COREY: The room blew up. I walked into it. Everyone came running. I stood in the doorway and I started barking orders. You—pull the fire alarm! You—get the kids out the doors! You—call the hospital, we need every ambulance in the county. And they went. Like a shot. Like I was an enormous shotgun. I felt—

SETH: Adrenaline.

COREY: I know adrenaline, I've been scared before. This—the whole place could have blown up and I could have taken it. I was...I was thrilled.

IRIS: *(Off)* Ann! See me in here, would you? *(She enters, carrying a pair of children's shoes in a plastic bag.)* No one seems to notice how their children are dressed. Last time they saw them alive and they can't picture them at all.

SETH: Corey. Would you excuse us, please?

(ANN enters.)

IRIS: These shoes don't match anyone's clothing list. Find out who they belong to.

ANN: How?

IRIS: Survivors are out there?

ANN: Yes.

IRIS: Show them the shoes.

SETH: It'll unhinge them.

ANN: There's blood on them.

IRIS: What do you want? We took the feet out.

SETH: Corey, it would be best if you left now.

COREY: No.

IRIS: If people give incomplete descriptions, they have to look at the actual effects. Serves 'em right.

SETH: The one who can identify them may be under sedation.

ANN: They're so little. Someone was proud to have tied these herself.

IRIS: Don't let your imagination get a mind of its own.

COREY: Those are Lydia's. She was proud of those shoes. She showed them off to everyone. Lydia Zuckerman.

IRIS: That's what we needed to know her by. Body 14. Good. One down.

SETH: You've got complete remains on this one?

IRIS: Enough to fill a coffin credibly. Closed coffin. *(To COREY)* Quick eye, there. Nice going.

(IRIS and ANN exit.)

SETH: You held together very well.

COREY: God, I must be detached. In my depths, you know? Down here. Down here I'm—

SETH: What's going on? Down there? Do you feel sick?

COREY: I must be sick, yeah, I must be one sick individual. It'll go away. *(Pause)* How recognizable are the children?

SETH: It varies wildly.

COREY: What if someone who knew them looked at them? To help the parents name them? So they wouldn't have to see so many. Would it spare them some pain?

SETH: You don't know what you're offering.

COREY: I've seen them. My memories of them are wrecked already.

SETH: If you're trying to help these children, spare yourself. Nothing we do and nothing we learn will ever save them. *(Pause)* I'll have to clear it with the others. Ann!

COREY: When people fight in wars, do they feel this way?

SETH: Some. The best ones.

COREY: What happens to them afterward?

(ANN enters.)

SETH: Would you get Iris and Sharon up here, please?

(ANN exits.)

SETH: I'll need you to wait outside while we talk this over.

COREY: Will you be there, too? Downstairs?

SETH: I'll be down there with you. I won't come up until you do.

COREY: I'll be in the hall. *(She turns to go.)*

SETH: Corey. Listen. I've had to learn what you're learning. There's a moment when you say, "All right. I decide on it. If I had it to do over, it would be what it is. This is what I actually wanted all along. Because I am not a victim things happen to. I am a person who learns. The more I can take in, the more complete I'll become. I will be a monster of knowledge. Let it all come."

(IRIS and SHARON enter.)

SETH: You might help us learn why they died.

COREY: Instead of me? I'd like to learn that. *(She exits.)*

SHARON: What are you up to?

SETH: I want her to look at the remains. The woman wants to help. And I think it'll help her.

SHARON: Help *her*? She is drunk with grief. Don't take advantage.

SETH: Think of all the false identifications it'll spare those pathetic people.

SHARON: Since when do you care about sparing anybody?

SETH: I'll take responsibility.

SHARON: I know you will.

SETH: She's tough.

SHARON: What are you, trying to build another of your own kind?

SETH: Iris? Should we let her see them?

IRIS: We've survived it. So can she.

SHARON: Oh, great. Solid advice from the Queen of the Dead.

(SETH *and* SHARON *laugh.*)

IRIS: Very funny.

(ANN *enters.*)

ANN: Excuse me—they can hear you out there.

SETH: Thanks, Ann. Sorry.

(SETH *and* ANN *exit.*)

SHARON: And he believed every word he said. He has no idea.

IRIS: God, that's frightening.

SHARON: Poor Seth.

IRIS: I liked her, too. She had a sharp eye.

SHARON: Poor thing.

IRIS: Well. Off we go.

(IRIS *and* SHARON *exit as the lights fade.*)

Scene Five

(FARSTED *is sitting at the table with his toolbox.* COREY *enters.*)

COREY: Farsted.

FARSTED: Corey.

COREY: What is that?

FARSTED: Belt sander. Don't see many this age still working.

COREY: What are you doing with it?

FARSTED: It's not working. Promised a man I'd have it for him. Fella refinishing thirty-five running feet of countertop, give me a couple days work. But this all happened and I'm supposed to be here, and I'm supposed to be there, so I thought I'd use the time. You don't think they'll care, do you?

COREY: No.

FARSTED: Some guys wouldn't bother, but you get known for conscientiousness, and there you are. Doing funny things.

COREY: What's the matter with it?

FARSTED: Belonged to my father, I think the bearings are fouled, he always took care of his tools, but you get a name for conscientiousness, you work in all weathers.

COREY: Let me see it. *(She takes the sander.)* Was your father conscientious, too?

FARSTED: He was a war hero. Before I was born. In combat you're conscientious or you're dead. He kicked back after that. Those bearings are in sad shape.

COREY: Yeah, the tracking's off. Give me a hunk of that steel wool, would you?

FARSTED: *(Passing a piece of steel wool)* Here you go. So what about my boy?

COREY: They're working on it. Lot of smart people in there. From the city? Quick.

FARSTED: What about you?

COREY: What about me?

FARSTED: I thought you'd be working on it. They were your class, right?

COREY: Right. Yeah, I'll be helping.

FARSTED: Nice for you.

COREY: How you figure?

FARSTED: Guys from the city. Successful.

COREY: You got some oil in there?

FARSTED: I'll shoot some. They know how they did it yet? The terrorists or whoever?

COREY: You think it was terrorists?

FARSTED: It's happening all over. Thought we'd be safe up here, raise the kids. Some guys would of left, go down and work for the aerospace. Lot of guys gone. Me, I thought—

COREY: Conscientious.

FARSTED: Keep the family out of the way, take care of my old man.

COREY: He died, didn't he?

FARSTED: Liver thing, took years. He was tough. Combat Marine.

COREY: There's a plug under here.

FARSTED: Got it. Try it out.

(COREY *guns the sander. She stares at the flying surface of the sandpaper as it runs down.*)

COREY: I've been having them do a unit on their grandparents for Show and Tell. (*She hands the sander back to* FARSTED.)

FARSTED: Did my boy do good in school?

COREY: He was very conscientious.

(*Pause*)

FARSTED: I'd better go back to that man's kitchen.

(FARSTED *exits.* COREY *stands and crosses downstage, singing under her breath.*)

COREY: She died of a fever
And no one could save her
And that was the end of sweet Molly Malone....
(*The faint hissing and knocking are heard, and repeat now and then.*) Today we'll
start our historical dioramas. To make a diorama you start with a shoe box
and you think of a picture of history. I'll give you an example of a diorama.
(*As she thinks for a moment, the light grows colder.*) There's a streetcorner in
the town where I went to school. Across the street from a little park with
a couple of trees. A little lawn. I remember a time I was standing there.
I'd always gotten a weird feeling at that corner—not always every time,
but often. It was 5:30 and it was the middle of the winter. I was about to
meet someone. (*She smiles.*) Yes, a boy. (*The smile fades.*) I was standing and
staring at a tree across the way. Thinking how black the tree was, full of
black leaves. And then there was a sound, and the tree shook and a whole
flock of birds rose out of it, hundreds of birds all of a sudden, this black
shape up in the sky, and left the tree behind. (*During the following, the three
women enter, wearing large white lab coats, their hands in their pockets.*) And I
felt like when I left that corner, and went where I was supposed to go next—
you know what it was? That I was looking at this world for the last time,
because when I left that corner and went where I was about to go, that the
world would be, I don't know, a different color from now on. So I stood
there. Yeah, pretty spooky. So I might take a shoe box and put in a little
person and a curb and a tree suddenly stripped of a skyful of birds, and
that's the way I'd make my diorama.

(SETH *enters and crosses down to her. They look at each other as the lights crossfade
to:*)

Scene Six

(One stark beam of light as from down a long hall. SETH *and* COREY *stand in the doorway. The three women are dimly visible.)*

SETH: Can you see what's in this room?

COREY: No.

SETH: Good. This is going to be a long bad day, and then it'll be over. Listen to me closely. There is a way of looking that I've learned. You can stare directly at them and barely see them at all. I'll tell you how to do it and when you're ready you'll turn on the lights.

COREY: I'll never get over this.

SETH: No. You'll get through it. Are you listening?

COREY: Go ahead.

SETH: In the explosion, it's as if their names, their identities have been thrown free of their bodies. So we look at the teeth, the fillings. We look at the bones, for old fractures. We get sex from the pelvis if intact. Race from the cheekbones and jaw and brow. The identification blows away. The fingerprints are the first to go. Hands and feet are so ephemeral. We're grateful for a face. This room contains information. Not people anymore. Remember that and you'll be fine.

COREY: Where's the light?

SETH: The switch is behind you. Feel?

COREY: Yes.

SETH: Whenever you're ready. To start with, concentrate on not seeing anything. Then see only what is here.

COREY: Their troubles are done.

SETH: Nothing but evidence.

COREY: Their troubles are done.

SETH: Nothing but information. There are no people here.

(A switch clicks. Moonlight on the three women.)

IRIS: Oh, my back.

SHARON: Big Dipper.

ANN: Where?

SHARON: See?

IRIS: Ursa Major.

SHARON: What?

ANN: Big Bear.

SHARON: How did they get a bear out of that?

IRIS: I wonder if they've moved since then?

ANN: The people?

IRIS: Which people?

ANN: Naming-things people.

IRIS: I wonder if the stars have moved.

SHARON: People haven't moved, we're where we've always been.

ANN: What are some other ones?

IRIS: Let's see....

ANN: The North Star, you go two up from which ones?

IRIS: I can't remember.

ANN: Those, I think. See?

IRIS: There's one like a "W" somewhere, where is that? Five stars together.

SHARON: Which are together and which are apart?

IRIS: Cassiopeia. There's a story about it.

SHARON: They all look together to me.

ANN: The night is so clear. There are so many.

SHARON: I don't see a "W."

ANN: What's the story?

IRIS: She's a queen in a chair and she can't get out of it. Her daughter's another constellation—do you remember the name? Something bad happens to her.

SHARON: The queen?

IRIS: Her daughter. But the queen has to watch.

ANN: In the sky.

SHARON: How do they get a queen in a chair out of five stars like a "W"?

ANN: How do you get a "W"?

SHARON: You find what you look for.

IRIS: Whoever named the stars was very morbid.

SHARON: They're millions of miles apart. They don't have anything to do with each other.

IRIS: They had powerful imaginations.

SHARON: I don't see a "W" at all.

IRIS: It's probably below the horizon this time of year.

ANN: They're beautiful.

IRIS: The light is very old, you know. It's energy from a long time ago. They could all be gone by now.

ANN: I don't understand how the light can be so bright when it's had to come so far.

SHARON: I think I'm getting cold.

IRIS: There's Orion.

SHARON: Where?

ANN: The Hunter.

IRIS: He's a belt and a sword.

ANN: I see him.

SHARON: Where?

IRIS: Follow my arm.

SHARON: There? Those?

IRIS: There.

SHARON: I see him! How about that.

(*The lights fade on the three women.*)

Scene Seven

(*The moon is down. As the scene goes on, it gets steadily darker, until* SETH *and* COREY *are visible only in silhouette.*)

SETH: Go home. Go to sleep.

COREY: I'm not tired, I wish I were tired, I'm not.

SETH: How do you feel?

COREY: Great, I should be struck dead for how I feel.

SETH: You've made all the difference. You're extraordinarily observant.

COREY: What kind of person—

SETH: You put yourself through hell—

COREY: I couldn't stop looking! Don't *thank* me. Christ. It was...fascinating.

SETH: You wanted to help. You hoped it would justify your survival. You did help. Others will suffer less. What are you ashamed of?

COREY: I thought I'd get rid of this—I thought by now—

SETH: What? Get rid of what? *(Pause)* All right. This may seem like a strange question, it may not: In a crisis like this, some people discover a physical desire. Not toward any object. Just a need. It would be completely normal. You almost lost your life. Your life is asserting itself. Or perhaps your case is different.

(Pause)

COREY: The longer this day goes on, the more I horrify myself.

SETH: Completely normal. Look. People have some surprising things inside them. And I don't mean the contents of their skins. You saw Iris and her staff taking all those photographs of the remains?

COREY: Thousands of them.

SETH: All those shutters clicking, sounded like a plague of locusts down there, didn't it? Several people on the staff collect those photographs.

COREY: As evidence.

SETH: They bootleg prints.

COREY: They collect them?

SETH: They keep scrapbooks. It's no good trying to stop them. They trade with their friends around the country, some of them. It's a hobby. Photos of notorious carnage.

COREY: Why? Why collect photographs of mutilated bodies?

SETH: They find it...fascinating.

COREY: I've got to ask you a question. You see these things all the time, you live with them in your head, you have friends and...a wife or whatever. You sleep and eat.

SETH: What's your question?

COREY: How?

SETH: How can I do this?

COREY: It's none of my business.

SETH: No, it's just...somebody has to, and I have a knack for it.

COREY: I'm keeping you from your work.

SETH: Do you want to go home?

COREY: I don't want to look at anything familiar right now.

SETH: We have beds set up here. Take one.

COREY: I'd better not. Seth, I've got to do something.

SETH: You've done something. You've survived.

COREY: I've got to do something else.

SETH: Is there someone you can call? A husband or whatever?

COREY: No, no husband or whatever. Not in this town. Men here...men here leave here. They go south and look for work building aircraft, or they stay in the mill and fester.

SETH: You're not from here?

COREY: Another little town, you wouldn't know its name.

SETH: I probably would.

COREY: My condolences. There was a job here, not many jobs in the world right now. What about you, are you married?

SETH: A long time ago, not anymore. There aren't many people where I work either.

COREY: You live in the city?

SETH: Once in a while.

COREY: How do people survive the speed of it? It must be exciting.

SETH: It can be...fascinating.

COREY: And you can go to the museum whenever you want.

SETH: Yes.

COREY: I would think that that would help. In my room, I have some postcards from the museum. I mounted them in old picture frames and hung them on the walls. They help me, sometimes.

SETH: Which artists? In your room?

COREY: Oh, Dürer, Vermeer. I think Dürer is just the right name for Dürer, don't you? Durable, endurance. Those firm lines.

SETH: Yes.

COREY: Vermeer is my great love. Those women working under open windows. I keep him in the kitchen, to remind me of the beautiful in the everyday.

SETH: Have you lived in the city?

COREY: I've always been drawn to it. I knew an artist from the city once. A boy. He painted me.

SETH: Did he.

COREY: One night we got very drunk on Burgundy wine, and he painted me. He started watercoloring my nails and kept on going and pretty soon I was festooned with watercolor. He was so gentle, camelhair brushes, so smooth. The only night of my life I've had camelhair on my skin. I thought I knew what a masterpiece would feel, so attended to, every millimeter of my surface attended to and thought out and eyed and touched. The colors didn't fade completely for weeks. I think I had to shed that entire set of skin before it went away. The—feeling you asked me about before.

SETH: Perfectly normal.

COREY: It might be back. I just wanted to warn you.

SETH: It's got nothing to do with me. You should try to sleep.

COREY: How can you live with this?

SETH: How do I live with myself? (Pause) I hope I'll do some good. I started in government because it seemed so graceful, when I was young, imposing harmony. Now I just try to contain the chaos. I'm supposed to learn the cause of this disaster. To keep it from happening again. But it won't happen again. These children won't die anymore. So all I can do.... Everyone, sooner or later, stands at a doorway and cries, "Someone I love is in there, let me in." And somebody has to say, no, you can't go in there. We strike a bargain. I'll never see her alive again. Can I settle for her dead? I'll give her a burial place. I'll give her a place in my memory. Is it a deal? Can I live with this? Stay sane? Keep working? Can I walk away? People like me—like us—our job is to stand in some doorway the dead have gone through, and turn the living back. No one will remember we were there. My days are full. But how I live with *myself*.... I guess what I hope is that I don't. You should go to sleep.

COREY: So should you.

SETH: It really would be wiser if we went to bed.

COREY: Each of us? Both of us? (Pause) I don't do this. It isn't me at all.

SETH: It isn't me either.

COREY: Your skin, it's like a child's. Here inside your wrist. So gentle. It's like it's never gone through anything.

SETH: Look, though. The veins and the bones come right through.

COREY: This baby skin wrapped around this old arm. Please would you open my blouse?

SETH: Would you like to move somewhere more comfortable?

COREY: No. The catch is in the front.

SETH: There we are. Beautiful.

COREY: I have inverted nipples. My breasts were my disappointment with my body, I'm afraid.

SETH: Not to me.

COREY: Now the—oh!

SETH: What?

COREY: Never mind, you found it for yourself.

SETH: Is that all right?

COREY: Yes. That's good. Something you should know. I've been told that I weep. If it happens, don't be scared, okay?

SETH: Okay.

COREY: Look into my eyes?

(Whatever light is left fades.)

END OF ACT ONE

ACT TWO

Scene One

(IRIS *and* ANN *are sitting at the table.*)

IRIS: Really?

ANN: Really. Please, I'm fascinated.

IRIS: Well. What I do is get to know all the people.

ANN: Do you divide them up among your team?

IRIS: You can't. That's the point. It has to be one mental picture. One mind, holding it all.

ANN: Like blindfold chess?

IRIS: Precisely. Precisely!

(SHARON *enters.*)

SHARON: Yes I'm late, sorry, let's get started. Where is he?

IRIS: We're waiting for him.

SHARON: Hey, I stop for his goddamn staff meetings, he can, too.

IRIS: He, uh—they haven't come down yet this morning.

SHARON: He and the—oy oy oy.

ANN: I guess this isn't like him? They talk about how driven he is.

IRIS: No, this is not like him.

SHARON: No. This *is* him. I've got facts to consolidate and he's off playing Hide the Body Part. (*She watches* ANN) She blushes. I love it.

IRIS: We were talking. Yes, it is like playing blindfold chess.

SHARON: Iris. Really?

ANN: Iris was telling me about mental pictures.

IRIS: Sculpture.

SHARON: I bet.

IRIS: The model for the identification of a group of bodies would resemble a three-dimensional transparent solid—

ANN: A glass cube?

IRIS: Yes. Gridded in all dimensions. One axis—across the top—would be the names of all the victims, Allen through Zuckerman. A second axis— say down the side—would be the numbers assigned to all the bodies, one through twenty-four. The third axis—the depth—it would be easiest to imagine as many sheets of glass, every sheet representing a trait.

SHARON: You figure that woman's a coroner groupie?

IRIS: Sharon, people are trying to hold a mental image here.

SHARON: Yeah, me, too. I don't see her as a coroner groupie though.

IRIS: This girl wants to learn something. Take a trait. Say, orthodontia.

ANN: Braces?

IRIS: Right. You talk to the families and find out which names wore braces. You look at the bodies, you see which are wearing braces. Each sheet of glass is a grid of squares. Each square represents the coordinate of a name and a body. If a square represents the conjunction of a braces name and a body with no braces, that's no good, and you black it out. If a square represents the conjunction of a body with braces and a name without, that's no good either, and you black *that* out. But if a square represents a name with braces and a body with braces, you leave the glass clear. Likewise if a square has an unbraced name and an unbraced body. You leave your square of glass transparent. You have a question?

ANN: What's a coroner groupie?

IRIS: A very rare pathological aberration.

SHARON: Death camp followers. The pillow talk defies description.

IRIS: Shut up, Sharon.

SHARON: One of them wanted to lie absolutely still while I—

IRIS: Shut up, Sharon.

ANN: You use a different plate of glass for each trait?

IRIS: Precisely. Thank you. Sex, if it can be determined—shut *up*, Sharon— eye color likewise; hair color, which you can look at subcutaneously even if the hairs themselves have burnt away. If there's a match between body and name, leave a clear space. Then when you have a deep enough axis of traits, you look at your solid and see where the light shines through. And there's your identity. Got it? Not that it's ever that simple in real life.

ANN: How can you get to know a roomful of dead people?

IRIS: Don't get superior.

ANN: I wasn't.

IRIS: They're dead and you're alive, and aren't you the uppity one.

ANN: Really, I didn't—

IRIS: Fear. That's all. Fear. Our goal is to be objective.

SHARON: Yeah. So much easier than being people.

IRIS: Don't knock objects. Objects were here before we were and they'll be here long after we're gone. In the meantime we exploit them. We make them more and more dangerous. Most of our work is viewing the result of a person losing an encounter with an object. And we always lose in the end.

(SETH *enters. They all look at him.*)

SETH: So. Morning.

SHARON: Thank you.

SETH: Staff meeting, five minutes.

SHARON: Yes, sir.

SETH: Shut up, Sharon. (*He exits.*)

ANN: May I ask you both a favor?

SHARON: Sure.

ANN: Would the two of you recommend that I be assigned to this section permanently? I did my internship in Parks and Recreation? This is a lot more interesting than Parks and Recreation, you know? This beats the hell out of Parks and Recreation.

(*The women remain as the lights change.*)

Scene Two

(IRIS, SHARON, *and* ANN *become* LUCY, ERINN, *and* GAIL. GAIL'*s head is on her hand, which covers one of her eyes.* FARSTED *enters, carrying a paper bag and drinking a beer. He crumples his beer can in his hands. He reaches into the bag, takes another beer and opens it.*)

LUCY: She's not a bad woman, really. Not spiteful.

ERINN: No?

LUCY: Just loose with herself.

ERINN: I didn't say cast her out. Live and let live. But that she can live, and others be taken away from us, that frets me terribly. Why was she spared? All those innocent children dead, and she of all people preserved.

LUCY: It's a miracle anyone survived.

ERINN: It's a senseless miracle. I've said it.

LUCY: She's very creative.

ERINN: Is that creativity? Dancing on the graves of children? People can be creative and still know right from wrong.

(COREY *enters. A long moment in which* COREY *feels no one speaking to her or acknowledging her presence.*)

FARSTED: How are you doing?

COREY: Bearing up.

FARSTED: Good. That's good.

COREY: And you?

FARSTED: I'm grieving. You know.

COREY: Gail. How are you?

(GAIL *lifts her head. She has a black eye.*)

COREY: Gail, what happened? Are you okay?

GAIL: Isn't it stupid? It's funny, when it happened I had a second there saying, "Oh great, my daughter's dead and now I'm going to have a black eye." It's the medication. Makes me goof up. Really really really stupid mistake with a cabinet door. Ben put in these cabinets?

COREY: How is Ben?

GAIL: They ought to give Ben some medication. Ha ha ha ha ha. See what he does then. He, boy, he just stood there, going, "Where's my little girl?" saying, "You had her last, where is she?" (*Touching the eye*) Cabinet door, boom. Stupid.

(*Pause*)

COREY: Lord above. Lucy?

(LUCY *turns to face her.*)

COREY: Are you still speaking to me?

LUCY: Could I see her?

COREY: Lucy, if you knew—an event like this—the condition of the remains—

LUCY: Was she blown to pieces? Just say so.

COREY: Yes.

(*Pause*)

LUCY: Back in the war they warned us in the factory what would happen if someone messed up. Put the fear of God in us girls. Seems wrong for it to happen to a little child.

COREY: Yeah.

ERINN: Corey? Can I ask you something?

COREY: Go ahead.

ERINN: You're not a God-fearing woman at all.

COREY: No.

ERINN: Think of that. Think of that. And He's killed my child.

COREY: And let me live.

ERINN: Yeah. Yeah, He did.

LUCY: Erinn. Honey.

COREY: And you think I'm happy about that.

ERINN: I've always tried to see His hand beneath my blessings. Blame the trials on Satan. I don't see what I could have done to bring this punishment down on that little boy. I doted on that boy.

COREY: They say He's jealous. He said so Himself.

(ERINN *slaps* COREY *across the face.*)

COREY: You're right. What a clever thing to say.

ERINN: Is that what it means. All my love, only for Him, leave your family, follow only Me. Well. That is petty. I'm sorry, but that is very small. If I have to love nothing in the world, or He'll take it from me, the way He has, again and again, He does this and says, "Turn to Me for comfort." Sick, in a way. I mean—is that what it meant, all along? Is that what He needs? That's pathetic. Men are His image, that's all I can say.

COREY: Have you thought He wanted your son with Him in heaven?

ERINN: You don't believe that.

COREY: No.

LUCY: I do, Erinn, I'm sure it's true.

ERINN: He didn't need that boy. He has angels galore. Spite. Spite. But I tell you: That boy had better be in heaven, because if he isn't, I'll go looking for him. I'll find him, too. I'll have all eternity to search in. I'll call his name from one end of it to the other, from the blackest pit up to God's own face, and if that boy doesn't have his just place, I'll see to it. I will set things right in heaven. Because I tell you: It's high time—high time—someone taught God about justice. (ERINN *exits.*)

LUCY: She didn't mean it.

COREY: Sure she did. I can't find any sense to it either. Me being here.

LUCY: Here in town?

COREY: I've been trying. Once we find out what happened, and I can get back in a classroom—

LUCY: Back in a classroom.

COREY: Well, I mean—that's what I do.

LUCY: Don't you think there might be questions about that?

COREY: What do you mean?

LUCY: Corey, I've always told everyone what a wonderful teacher you are, but.... Do you think there are any classrooms free? The town doesn't have much money as it is, we can't just put you in an empty classroom, which is what we'd have to do, because, I mean, there's one less group of students in the school now, and it was yours.

COREY: Do you think—do you really think they would—

LUCY: Maybe it would be easier somewhere else?

COREY: I'm the teacher whose class blew up. It's going to make for an ambiguous letter of recommendation.

LUCY: There must be something else you can do?

COREY: I've got no system but the school system.

LUCY: There might be a way, after this blows over—

COREY: No. You're saying that now, but a second ago you said the opposite. They'll never let me back—

LUCY: Corey, I'd better check on Erinn, she—

COREY: —this is the last classroom I'll ever see, this one here, when I walk out of here, I won't know where to put myself, because the thing is—the thing—the thing is that I teach.

LUCY: Corey, I have to go.

COREY: What do you want me to do?

LUCY: I'm sure you'll think of the right thing. (She exits.)

COREY: What do you want me to do?!

(Pause)

FARSTED: You want a beer?

COREY: What?

FARSTED: We could go outside if you wanted to.

COREY: Now? I'm—

FARSTED: Sit, drink a beer. Right outside. You'd hear him call.

COREY: Where's your wife?

FARSTED: She's down the hall with people watching her. They've given her something so she doesn't scream anymore. She chuckles a lot. Does it by the hour. Where's your government man? *(Pause)* Nobody's holding anything against each other, huh? Would I be talking to you? Offering you a beer?

COREY: Why are you?

FARSTED: I thought—a time like this, people know each other better. You got troubles, I got troubles. You knew my boy, we could talk about my boy. What I'm asking—how do you talk to that guy? What did you say so he knew what you wanted?

COREY: I don't want to drink on the ground. Sitting on the dirt and drinking, that's too sad.

FARSTED: We're supposed to be sad. Come on, if he said, "Let's take a seat here on the lawn and drink champagne," you'd go. I can see why you'd do that.

COREY: Can you?

FARSTED: I'm trying to. I mean—what have you got there? Is he your ride out of here or what?

COREY: He's learning things. Some people do that.

FARSTED: I need to learn something. Can you teach me something?

COREY: I should leave.

FARSTED: We could both leave. You want to leave? I'll walk you.

COREY: You're scaring me, Farsted. All right?

FARSTED: I'm not trying to scare you, I need to ask you something!

COREY: Why are you threatening me?

FARSTED: I'm sitting here. I haven't raised a hand. I'd never.

COREY: I don't know that.

FARSTED: You got powerful friends. Squash me like a snail on the sidewalk, that guy.

COREY: He's here to learn what happened is all.

FARSTED: Yeah. Yeah. So you talk to him. You two are probably so good at talking that's all it takes. You get good enough at doing a thing. Guys I know—you know too, I won't name who, don't want to tempt you—guys fix up a car so good, they do it *that* way. Muscle car, put a woman on the passenger side, go fast enough, get those low vibrations. They tell me, I wouldn't know—they have to hose down the seats after? Talking, this guy, same way I bet.

COREY: You're hurting me, Farsted, why?

FARSTED: I'm asking a question. You and him, you—talk. Information rubs off. So maybe you know how things like—with these dead bodies. What's the rule?

COREY: What rule?

FARSTED: I don't know, I'm asking you. If somebody's got dead bodies, how long are they allowed to keep them?

COREY: How long are they allowed—

FARSTED: Or anybody. Anybody with dead parts. Do they get in trouble?

COREY: Will he get in trouble?

FARSTED: Or anybody.

COREY: I don't understand what you're asking.

FARSTED: I'm trying to learn something and I don't know what it is.

COREY: If somebody holds onto dead bodies—

FARSTED: Or parts even.

COREY: Will somebody get in trouble if they hold onto dead body parts for a long time?

FARSTED: You did it. That's the thing I don't know.

COREY: I don't know either. How long are we talking about?

FARSTED: Say years. Years and years for instance.

COREY: I don't think it'll take him anything like that long.

FARSTED: You never know.

COREY: I could ask. I could try to learn for you.

FARSTED: No, no, don't try to learn for me. I was hoping you'd know. *(He exits.)*

GAIL: I'm sorry. I fell asleep. Did they all go? I'm sorry. I saw you. Last night. When I opened the door. I saw you sleeping.

COREY: Sleeping.

GAIL: It looked like you were. He was sleeping. I didn't mean to. I just opened the wrong door, I'd been over getting another pill, and I was walking back, and these pills keep making me do stupid things with doors.

COREY: And you saw me.

GAIL: Both of you. Afterward, I guess. Asleep, all—together.

COREY: Gail. You told them, didn't you?

GAIL: I never tell. Oh, the—what I saw.

COREY: Why?

GAIL: I guess—I must have had to.

COREY: Yeah.

GAIL: I'm sorry.

COREY: It happens. Why don't you go back to sleep now.

GAIL: Thanks. I hope so.

COREY: Were you dreaming?

GAIL: No. It was nice. Just—no.

(COREY *exits.* GAIL *lowers her head. The lights fade.*)

Scene Three

(SETH *is working at the table.* COREY *enters.*)

COREY: I need to ask you something.

SETH: Hi.

(They embrace.)

COREY: Listen. People know.

SETH: And they're unhappy about it.

COREY: Oh boy.

SETH: And this matters to you.

COREY: They think I don't care what happened to their children. It was bad enough I'm alive, but now.... I know these people. I should have known how they expect you to behave in a disaster. I did know.

SETH: You tried. You couldn't act that way.

COREY: I'll never get them to understand this, I can't tell them the truth, they'll never want to hear it, they'd rather I just—they'd rather not have to look at me. Everyone I meet—they look at me—and I don't make any sense. I'm sorry. This is not even slightly fascinating. It's just—Farsted was out there ranting at me about parts of the body. Saying somebody might get in trouble. It was crazed, it was very deeply crazed. I guess he's been unhappy in his family a long time. But he's never.... *(Pause)* I think I know something.

SETH: Tell me.

COREY: I don't know if I should. I don't want to be wrong about this.

SETH: Tell me.

COREY: I wanted them to love history, so they would learn it. I thought, who do children love better than their grandparents?

SETH: Their grandparents are history in person....

COREY: Their grandparents have saved things from the past.

SETH: Souvenirs.

COREY: I said, if you're very careful, and get permission, this is what we'll do in Show and Tell.

SETH: Whose turn was it that day to bring things in?

COREY: Tommy Farsted.

SETH: Whose grandfather was—

COREY: A war hero.

SETH: A souvenir is an object charged with time. If matter is energy in a different state, is time energy, too? Burning so slowly. We didn't identify any of the bodies as Tommy Farsted. He isn't here.

COREY: He ran away. He brought something in and ran away.

SETH: This still doesn't make enough sense, it still doesn't account for all of the damage. Christ. I'm going to have to put it all back together, aren't I? All right then. *(He refers to photographs and charts on the table. He moves around the room, acting out with an arm or a leg the moves he describes.)* Would it be possible that—if her arm ends up there—

(As SETH *mentally replaces the bodies where they fell,* COREY *watches them die.)*

COREY: Lydia—

SETH: —and the torso—

COREY: Christopher—

SETH: —here. Turned this way? Explosion! I'm spun so, hit that tow-headed—

COREY: Kenny—

SETH: —desk fragment—is there?—*that* one, the legs to the knee—

COREY: Greta—

SETH: —flies *across*, takes the arm and spine—

COREY: Cyndi—

SETH: —so, the torso underneath—

COREY: Robby—

SETH: —here. But explain the disembowelment of this one.

COREY: Katey—

SETH: I explain it thus: *(He begins his dance of death, flying around the room, the impacts more and more violent.)* I'm here. Facing front, no, back to the *that's* right. Piece of the desk, edge on, lumbar-to-hips flies like—

COREY: Phillip—

SETH: —rips in this direction, flight path, *so*, legs across the—

COREY: Nancy—

SETH: —Yes of course, and thus the crumpled heap—

COREY: Steve—

SETH: Now. What did this? Could it be—whose is this? Who does this belong to? No, no, clearly, look—she's embedded in that one—

COREY: Paul—

SETH: —facing that way, why is this one facing away?

COREY: Cath—

SETH: Sees what's coming? Scared? Anthropomorphic garbage, the *pieces*, eyes on the *pieces*. Look, here, see what you know. The Asian girl.

COREY: Lynn—

SETH: Taken, into the wall, hence the—head—

COREY: Dan—

SETH: —foot—

COREY: Ben—

SETH: —pelvic—

COREY: Curt—

SETH: —*yes*, so *what* made the, this, and here, and all the— shrapnel, no, debris, no, another body, maybe, but where *is* it? All right. Where would it have had to be?

(SETH *moves with a new urgency.* COREY *begins to walk slowly toward a particular spot.*)

COREY: Tommy?

SETH: Let's say here, standing behind the—explosion! No, there'd be some of me here. Standing on top of—explosion! No, the ceiling, did they check—nothing in the ceiling here so—

COREY: Tommy?

(SETH *has arrived very close behind* COREY.)

SETH: Here. Right smack *here*, I'm—what if I'm—

COREY: Holding the mine.

SETH: *(Grasping her in his arms)* Yes!

COREY: *Finish it.*

SETH: I'm cradling it, I'm that close, with it, showing it, I've brought this to show you, oh my God he blew up in their faces! I'm Farsted, it's my turn, I've put them in a wagon, dragged them in, picked up this land mine. Look. See. A few get scared, a few move toward me. Maybe I slip—maybe I pull something—maybe I've never been very happy in school. So Farsted is here, and I'm Farsted—explosion! I'm blown to bits. Yes! Done it!

(COREY *sobs in terrible pain as* SETH *holds her.*)

COREY: All gone all gone all gone all gone all gone...

SETH: Ann!

(ANN *enters.*)

SETH: Have Mr Farsted brought in. Tell Iris and Sharon to come up. And tell them to bring that old flesh they found.

(ANN *exits.*)

COREY: Not one of them absent. Not one. All gone. When I teach...when I taught. On the good days, we all—oh, the energy flies, your body tingles, you could almost smell the ozone. The children store that energy, they can run on it for years. All gone. It never occurred to me—I put something in his mind. It started ticking. That was the cause of this whole thing. My cause.

SETH: Stop now.

COREY: My great cause.

SETH: Stop. Tommy Farsted had four grandparents. What caused him to want to tell about this one? What caused the explosion in your classroom instead of somewhere else along the way? It could have been the street, it could have been the hallway. Corey, don't take this on. Believe me. Please believe me. There's no reason to it.

(COREY *removes herself from his arms.*)

COREY: I should go home. Those people need you to be done.

SETH: Where are you going?

COREY: I said I'd stay here long enough to learn what happened. Now I've learned. I know my mistakes. That Show and Tell assignment, that was one mistake. And leaving the room. I'll never make that mistake again. So now I know. Thank you.

(ANN *enters.*)

SETH: For what?

COREY: For answering my question.

SETH: Which question was that?

COREY: The reason I'm not dead. You're right. There's no reason at all.

SETH: When I'm finished here, I'll come find you. All right? Corey? All right?

(*She's gone.*)

ANN: Seth. They're ready for you.

SETH: Right, thanks...

(ANN *exits.* SETH *gathers his papers.*)

SETH: Good work...

(*As* SETH *exits, the lights fade.*)

Scene Four

(COREY *is pacing, feeling the air with a still hand. The hissing sound is much louder. Behind the table the three women are sitting, dimly visible. Light shows around the door, and grows brighter through the rest of the scene. Three loud knocks.*)

COREY: Science. Remember the experiment we did with the candle in the bottle? Where as long as the flame was alive it kept poisoning and poisoning the air in the bottle until the flame put itself out? Remember how we had to make sure there weren't any leaks, or it wouldn't work? This is like that. A room is a container, like a bottle, or a box. Doors sealed, windows sealed. Think of your body as a bottle with your self inside. (*Three loud knocks, and "Corey" called faintly*) And once you've done all that, you can wait, and look at your Vermeer. If you stare a long time, the people in the painting seem to breathe. Long after we've stopped, they'll still be seeming that way. *(Three loud knocks)* He's painted an open window, and you think, I should close that window, or this won't work. But you can't. That window's going to be open forever. *(She shakes her head and sinks to her knees.)* So it's good. You sit in front of your painting, and feel the breeze in your face. It's all right. *(Pounding now, three times, and "Corey!" called more loudly)* Wait a minute. The breeze in your—no. Fresh air, that isn't right. You don't want fresh air. You want to leave the gas on. Huh. There's a trick to killing yourself. You have to learn everything backwards. I've never heard that. That's interesting. I bet there's a lesson in that. *(She tries to stand and sinks back.)* I should teach that to people. They'll be interested. Oh, right. I'll be dead. *(Pounding, three times. "Corey!")* Wait. Somebody's out there. *(She looks toward the source of the pounding.)* If I open the door, I could tell them.

(Pounding, five times, as the lights fade)

Scene Five

(SETH, SHARON, and IRIS are around FARSTED at the table.)

SETH: Please, Mr Farsted.

FARSTED: I don't know.

SETH: Mr Farsted, we have the truth already, all we want from you is confirmation. I'll ask you again: Do you want a lawyer?

FARSTED: No lawyer.

SETH: He'd be someone on your side.

FARSTED: Who picks him?

SETH: The government.

FARSTED: Who pays him?

SETH: The government. But he'd be on your side.

FARSTED: No. Thank you.

SETH: Mr Farsted, your friends and neighbors—the parents of your son's classmates—they are desperate for answers. Please don't make them wait any longer.

FARSTED: I just don't know.

SETH: All right, then. Sharon?

(SHARON holds up the bag of brown stuff.)

SHARON: I want to show you something, Mr Farsted. Have you ever seen these before?

FARSTED: I don't know.

SHARON: Do you know what they are?

FARSTED: I can't tell.

SHARON: We found these bits of old flesh. We were able to reconstruct a couple of them. *(She shows him a smaller bag.)* Look. Can you tell what that is?

FARSTED: I'm not sure.

SHARON: Name it! I want to see your stupid mouth make its name!

FARSTED: Ear.

SHARON: What?

FARSTED: It's an ear.

SHARON: Is it? It's got a hole in it. See? This one does, too. Not here... *(Her finger approaches his ear.)* ...where the sound goes into the head. Not here... *(Her finger nearly touches his earlobe.)* ...where you might have it pierced for decoration. But here.

(She touches the upper part of his ear. He jerks his head away.)

SHARON: They're all like that. And this piece here, what is this?

FARSTED: Wire. Through the hole.

IRIS: They're—

SHARON: From his mouth.

FARSTED: Trophy necklace.

SHARON: What?

FARSTED: His trophy necklace.

SHARON: Whose?

FARSTED: My father was a hero.

(Pause)

SETH: With a hero's decorations.

FARSTED: They were all put away.

SHARON: Why didn't you turn them in, report them—

FARSTED: They weren't doing any harm. You call somebody official, you tell them you've got bombs, you're in trouble. Sir, my Daddy was a hero.

SETH: Could your son have been hoping to learn how his grandfather could be a hero and do terrible things like this?

FARSTED: This...I always thought there was a warrior's code. Soldiers from both sides did it. Always have.

SHARON: Madness. Insanity.

SETH: People drive themselves insane when they feel it's expected of them. So they can do our terrible things. Could that be why your son brought them to Show and Tell? So he could learn how to feel about it?

FARSTED: Feel about what?

SETH: That he was on this earth thanks to atrocities. His grandfather survived and had you, and you had him. How could he be a fair exchange for all those people's blood? Maybe he wanted to know.

FARSTED: He was nine years old.

SETH: I want to know. Don't you?

FARSTED: I don't dwell on it.

SETH: We all dwell on it. It is the question we dwell on. I wonder how long ago he found that footlocker. I wonder how long he waited to find someone—someone like Corey—who might help him understand what it meant. *(Beat)* Mr Farsted, we'll be turning our findings over to the governor. You'd better prepare your family.

FARSTED: If I could—is there any chance of getting my son, at this time?

SETH: I'm afraid not.

FARSTED: I don't see why you have to keep punishing him, Sir, I don't see why you can't just let me take him home.

SETH: Mr Farsted—

FARSTED: Or it's because of these ears, I guess, but listen, you know all about remains, I didn't know who to *start* to ask before, but if you told me what I should do, what would be proper and fitting, I would do it right now.

SETH: Mr Farsted—

FARSTED: I guess people's little children get blown up all the time now. But these ears from a half-century-ago soldiers, that's really bad, I guess. But when you inherit a house, you know, all paid, decent furniture, stuff you grew up with, all belongs to you, one little footlocker, way back in the basement, everything else is good, nice town. Show me one person who would drive away and leave that. Some people would of called up the officials and said, "Look at this bad thing my Daddy had." Some people would of sold that house, tried to leave that footlocker behind for somebody else maybe. Some people aren't conscientious at all.

IRIS: Mr Farsted, we would give you your son if we could. I couldn't find him. The cause of an event this extreme tends almost to vanish. He was probably holding up a landmine to show everyone. There's nothing left. Mr Farsted, I looked and looked.

SETH: No one blames your boy. Every child goes down to a basement and opens a box and thinks he's finally found the secret that everyone is keeping. What Tommy did, one way or another, everyone does. We couldn't find him, but we recognize him. We'd know him anywhere. You may return to your home, Mr Farsted.

(FARSTED *exits.*)

SHARON: I get too angry. I take too much out on them.

IRIS: Mr Farsted kept some objects connected with death. I don't think the three of us are in a position to condemn him.

SETH: I should go see Corey.

(ANN *enters.*)

SETH: Ann, good, assemble the press.

ANN: They've all gone. I came to tell you.

SETH: No. Oh, no.

ANN: An air disaster. Hundreds of casualties. Passengers and onlookers.

SHARON: How did it happen?

ANN: All they know is hundreds of holiday travelers caught fire and fell from the sky.

IRIS: Hundreds? Two? Five?

ANN: Closer to five, I think.

IRIS: Terrible.

SHARON: Senseless tragedy.

ANN: That's what I came in to tell you, a call came from the Capitol. We have to catch a plane straight there.

SHARON: We'll have to write the report on this one on the way.

IRIS: Hundreds. Closer to five. And a name to learn for every one. Off we go.

SETH: I need to see if Corey's okay, I owe her an—

SHARON: Seth. People must be grieving by the thousand.

(*They exit as the lights fade.*)

Scene Six

(COREY *enters. She glances downstage.*)

COREY: Hi, what's the matter? (*She crouches as if to speak to a child at a little distance away, down front.*) What happened to you? Show me? Hm. Can you stop crying? Okay, you cry a little longer, then. Uh-huh? You'll have a handsome scab, there. You'll be able to pick at that for a couple of weeks. Sure you can pick at it. You should only do it if you want to get a scar, though. You could get a tough-looking scar out of that. Hey, you stopped crying, did you notice? Yeah, you'll live.

(SETH *enters.*)

SETH: Corey?

(COREY *stands.*)

SETH: Corey, Jesus, I'm glad to see you. They said you'd be here, but—
I was afraid you might disappear again. You really disappeared, you know?
You wouldn't believe how many people I've had out looking for you.

COREY: Seth. You didn't have to do that.

SETH: I only wanted to be sure you were all right—

COREY: I'm all right. I'm functioning. There's nothing more you have to do.

SETH: The second we finished, they took and threw me into this—it went on for miles, it was a whole landscape of—my work. I kept trying to get away to find you, and when I finally did, you were gone.

COREY: You're going to get me in trouble, someone from the government showing up asking questions. It's my first day here, I'm nervous enough as it is.

SETH: Listen. This may seem like a strange question, but.... Would you consider coming with us? You don't have to do anything, if you don't want to. Just be there. We can travel around the state together. I'll take you to all the worst places.

COREY: Seth. I'm a teacher.

SETH: You could work with the survivors if you wanted to. Find the exceptional ones, and teach them. Teach them how to look at things.

COREY: Seth...

SETH: Right. Stupid idea. I just thought.... Corey, people like us are hard to find. You'll find it gets lonely, out here. It would be good to be...adjacent to someone.

COREY: They can't find anyone who's willing to teach here. I think they barely checked my background, they were so happy to have me. They said, you don't want to work in this school, we have to warn you, it's dangerous here. *(She laughs softly.)*

SETH: May I ask you a question?

COREY: Of course.

SETH: You got out. You walked away.

COREY: What's your question?

SETH: How?

COREY: I learned so much that day. It nearly killed me. And the next day I learned something else. And I about left myself for dead. But another day came, and I picked up another fact or two. And how I come to be here is, I could not stop learning. Live people learn. So I'm here.

SETH: You're right. I learn something every day. But you know? Day after day I learn the same damn thing.

(A school bell rings.)

COREY: I have to go. My class will be waiting for me.

SETH: I'm glad I got to see...that you're here. I'm grateful.

COREY: So am I.

(SETH exits. COREY watches him out of sight. She crosses downstage and claps her hands.)

COREY: Class. Good morning, class. My name is Corey, and I'll be your substitute. Could someone open up those curtains, please? You and you, thank you. Let's have some sunlight here. *(The light brightens. Her eye is caught by something at slightly above eye height, downstage. Her eyes widen, but she goes on.)* Now I'll need you to tell me how far along in your texts you are. But first things first. *(She crosses behind the table, and picks up an autoharp case. She holds it briefly, and places it on the table. She looks up again.)* I always like to start with music. And so... *(She opens the case and gently lifts out an autoharp.)* This is an autoharp. It's not a fancy musical instrument. It sounds pretty lonely unless it's helping someone sing. *(She looks up again.)* Please excuse me, it's just that it's my first day, and I came up from another direction, so I didn't know. Who can tell all of us what that is? That white...building. That's right. That's the Capitol building. I had no idea it was so close. Well. Let's sing a song. I'm sure you know it, so I'll go through it for you and you join me when you're ready. *(As she plays the chords, she looks up.)* Think about all the important people sitting up there, working so hard, trying to keep things orderly. Don't you think they ought to hear you sing? They'll look up from their work and say, "Who is making all that beautiful noise?" *(Singing)*

Crying cockles and mussels
Alive, alive oh

Alive, alive oh
Alive, alive oh
Crying cockles and mussels,
Alive, alive oh...

(The lights fade.)

END OF PLAY

CPSIA information can be obtained
at www.ICGtesting.com
Printed in the USA
LVHW020904020421
683299LV00004B/182